# Alive on a
# Rainy Day

*The front cover is from an original water-colour painting commissioned by the author. It was the work of his friend the late Noel Messenger, who illustrated those books of the author which were published by the Swanhill Press. This painting depicts a boat fishing party caught in a squall whilst harling for salmon on the Lower Tay before the Great War.*

*The drawings inside are by another talented artist, Keith Linsell, who illustrated Geoffrey's earlier books. Keith also painted the splendid picture on the front cover of the First Edition.*

# Alive on a Rainy Day

## or

## *Fishing is a Way of Life*

Geoffrey Bucknall

*Revised second edition*

BRIGHT WATER PRESS

First published in the United Kingdom in 2009 by
Bright Water Press, Postgate Cottage, Lartington, DL12 9DA
ISBN 978–0–9562552–1–1

Produced by
The Choir Press
Gloucester, GL1 5SR

Retail and trade enquiries for this book should be addressed to:
Coch-Y-Bonddu Books
Machynlleth, Powys, SY20 8DG

# DEDICATION

This book is dedicated to the memory of my late friend, Henri Limouzin. We were friends for over fifty years. He was 'Froggie' and I was 'Rosbif'. We had views in common about life, literature, religion, politics and even fishing. So we could never have a proper discussion about anything. He loved this book. He died suddenly whilst translating it for a French publisher.

I am fishing on Cow Green reservoir with my friend, Mike Robinson. As it is July in the high Pennines, it's raining stair-rods. I say to my companion, 'Mike, it's pissing down with rain and cold enough to freeze the balls off a brass monkey. I'll be glad when I've had enough of this.'

'For Chrissake stop your bellyaching,' he replies. 'There are plenty of folk in the cemetery who'd be pleased to change places with you. It's better to be alive on a rainy day than dead on a sunny one.'

*Geoff returns a healthy twenty-pound pike he caught on legered herring bait in Longford Lake, near Sevenoaks, Kent.*

# Acknowledgements

It is my practice to acknowledge sources in the text and in footnotes. To list them again would be unnecessary duplication.

There are a small number of books which helped me to develop my own fishing philosophy. At the risk of duplication I would say that the major influence on my fishing life was Bernard Venables. At a time when specimen hunting became the dominant influence in our sport with the creation of single-species clubs, BV persuaded me that the greatest pleasure was to fish for anything, anywhere. His philosophy took me from village roach ponds to eel fishing on the dykes of the Romney Marsh, then on to fly fishing for trout and the years of boat fishing in coastal waters. He also encouraged me to put pen to paper for his splendid *Creel* magazine. His was a voice of sanity in a time when angling was going slightly mad. When size of the capture became everything, encouraging the artificiality which dominates stocking policy and, perhaps, future genetic engineering, our sport needed a writer of distinction to remind us what our values should be. When many anglers were besotted with the idea of catching the largest specimens of a single species, he reminded them that the sport offers far more enjoyment than taking the stress of competitive modern life with them to the water-side. This is what he taught me.

Geoff Bucknall

# 1

*As I went down to Dymchurch Wall*
*I heard the South sing o'er the land*
*I saw the yellow sunlight fall*
*On knolls where Norman churches stand.*
John Davidson, 'In Romney Marsh'

IN 1966 I wrote my first book, called *Fishing Days*. It was about growing up before the war, fishing rod in hand, and my subsequent career as an angler. Since then I have given talks and been on many fishing expeditions and I am flattered to be presented by collectors with copies of my books to sign. Recently in Caithness, whilst signing a pile of books, I came across a copy of *Fishing Days* and idly I enquired how much it had cost. 'Eighty pounds,' was the startling reply. 'Why are they charging so much?' I asked. 'Oh, the dealers believe you to be dead.'

*Fishing Days* was the first book I wrote, though not the first published. You may think it to have been presumptuous to have written an autobiographical book at such an early age when I was completely unknown in sporting circles. I owe you an explanation.

You see, at that time I was struck down with a duodenal ulcer, which is a pain like a bayonet thrust through the abdomen to the left shoulder. In those days, before the miracle drugs, sufferers were put to bed for a few weeks on a reducing diet of such delights as eggnogs, boiled fish and tepid milk. Between bouts of agony came periods of boredom, so my wife suggested I write a book. She encouraged me by buying me a small portable typewriter. What subject?

1

The only thing I knew was fishing, the virus having entered my blood from the age of seven, never leaving me free again to this day. So I set to work; the pages piled up. On recuperation I stored the manuscript in a drawer and forgot it, never dreaming that it would ever appear between hard covers in book shops.

I had to decide what sort of a fishing book to write. I did decide to write this book to please myself, and when I broke this rule with one or two subsequent books, written to commission, I was never pleased with the result. I am down-right ashamed of one I churned out in a few weeks when I needed cash in a hurry.

I wrote *Fishing Days* for fun. I am writing this book for fun. It is the only way to write.

An autobiography has to be based on a personal philoso-phy. Aye, 'there's the rub'. I had none. Worse, I did not even know what 'philosophy' meant. Truth to tell, I discovered accidentally the meaning long after my seventieth birthday, in this wise. My family has a dash of French blood in its veins and I was encouraged when young to be vaguely bilingual. It makes sense to defer the ageing process by keeping active body and mind, so I signed up for a French literature course in the City, fondly imagining that I would be swashbuckling with Cyrano or inspecting murdered corpses with Maigret. Unhappily the young Prof. plunged us into Sartre and Exis-tentialism, about which I knew nothing. I asked a fellow student in the next desk, shrouding my mouth to a whisper, 'What the hell does existentialism mean?' After a pause she replied, 'I think it means that you can do what you bloody well like.'

Of course schoolboys in France have philosophy as a compulsory subject, and they are on nodding terms with Heidegger who I thought was a striker for Munich. Later in this book I shall tell you about my frustrating search for a personal philosophy, but at that time I had none unless you can include the problem of fitting cricket, motorbikes, cider and girls into a busy fishing life.

It goes without saying that autobiographies are also based on memories. If you visit your local library you will see hefty political memoirs gathering dust, but they are not true to memory since they are engineered to defend the indefensible. The public knows this. If there were such a thing as an honest autobiography it would include all memories, the good, the bad and the ugly. All of our lives are mixtures of these.

A boy born long before the last war, unless he came from a privileged family, would have lived in stark times. Most schools, including the first elementary school to which I went in the Kentish Weald, had a pecking order of physical brutality where boys were beaten according to strength and size, right up to the headmaster who beat everyone without fear or favour. It was a time of unemployment and privation. Let me give you an example, so much better than a catalogue of statistics of the thirties.

Not so long ago my younger son and I went on a fishing trip to Shetland where we rented a cottage in an isolated community. On stashing our gear into the drawers we found an ancient school photograph. The pupils were lined up in the usual rows for the camera. Simon was puzzled that none of the kids wore shoes; they were all barefoot. A memory flooded back. My father, the village schoolmaster of that time, also arranged the school photograph, and since some children came to school barefoot, he made all of the rest remove their shoes and boots.

Why mention this? It has nothing to do with fishing? It does, you see, for to write a book about your life without an underlying philosophy, you needs must set a tone. This means that memory has to be selective. As fishing is my life, I decided to write *Fishing Days* as a sunny book. The events, perhaps somewhat romanticised, would be happy, but true.

In memories of life and fishing, where possible, I want the sunshine to be on the water.

Trouble is that in retrospect I feel guilty. I ignore a society that was stratified. When I tried to tell my children of the sort of world in which I grew up I realised that to them it was an unknown, boring planet, a yawn. I sat in a school-room where a huge map of the world showed vast areas coloured in red. The sun never set on the Union Jack.

The natives woke up one day under *Pax Britannica* to discover that they had Christianity and cricket whilst Britain had the land. To prove that fishing and the larger world are inextricably meshed together, colonials were able to fish the pure dry fly for trout in Kenya and Kashmir, to hunt the mighty mahseer in India and the 'Tigris salmon' in Mesopotamia. I recollect that the worst book on fishing I ever read was written by a Colonel in India to advise newcomers how to catch mahseer. As a shikari (a sort of cross between a servant and a ghillie) could be too excitable after the fishing started, he advised that he should be put into a tied-up sack and left on the bank. The House of Hardy provided special tackle for mahseer fishing, so you see 'the Empire' did have an angling input.

Those of us who endured hard times in the war often sneer at the post-war generations, mollycoddled on free orange juice, milk and cod liver oil. Made them soft. When I went pike fishing with one such product of the Welfare State, I found that he could not drag his quivering flesh from beneath the bedcovers of the Pleasure Boat Inn on Hickling Broad when the first light of a February dawn was peeping over a frozen horizon. The ducks were already squabbling on the staithe below our windows. In vain did I tell him that Mistress Esox went early to breakfast and late to supper. I thought that 1929-born men like me, we resembled pre-war cars; may not have had the speed, but we did have the stamina. I suppose our forefathers, who served in the ranks in Foreign Service, would have sneered at us, for that which they gained for Empire we gave up after the war was over.

That social stratification was also reflected in angling. There was a clear division between coarse fishermen and game anglers, especially when the latter were the purists of the dry fly. Like all generalisations it was not true of the whole of Britain. In those days they said that 'God could not get a rod on the Test.' There was the occasional exception, a 'parvenu', usually a retired bookie from humble stock who wore a loud check suit, brown boots and bowler hat, and who never removed the band from his cigar just to show how expensive it was. I wonder if he escaped the blackball of the Fly Fishers' Club? Did he fish the Test and the best salmon rivers of Scotland? Or did he infiltrate after the war, I wonder? But fly fishing had working-class roots in the North, though it was the despised block-and-tackle down-stream wet variety, lacking the sophistication of 'exact imitation'.

These things went through my mind when writing *Fishing Days*. So, yes, I decided to write a sunny book, a happy book with humorous anecdotes. I think it reflected a side of my nature that is cheerful and optimistic, to which depression has been a stranger. And it was true, though selective. Now, in my eighties, the problems are different. 'The ceremony of innocence is drowned', as Yeats described the growing-up process. I can only promise you this: I will remain true to memory, I will try to entertain with sunny episodes, but I cannot entirely scour from these pages comment on how the sport has changed in my lifetime, how it reflects changes in society. Attitudes are different now, if only because the sense of community in hard times has devolved onto Government ... our brother is no longer our keeper, but Big Brother keeps a vigilant watch.

Forgive me; I had no philosophy of life when I wrote *Fishing Days*. There was no such intrusion in that book. A book writer has to make choices. Are such choices free? Damn that introduction to Sartre! He told me: 'Man is condemned to be free.' We have to make agonising decisions in life. I see him now, sitting outside his bistro in Paris, glass of vin rouge in hand, gaulois stuck on his lower lip as he eyes up the passing young ladies. Then came the contradiction in Dr William Sargant's book, *Battle for the Mind: a Physiology of Religious Conversion and Brain-Washing*. He makes the convincing case that none of our decisions is free. Neither the big ones, nor the small ones, as between tea or coffee. They are all predetermined for us by subconscious influences, upbringing and environment, as if we were Pavlov's dogs. Our choices can only be changed by terror, abreaction and brainwashing. I wonder, for there were no fishermen in my family. Did I choose fishing as a way of life? No, rather did fishing choose me.

How did it start, how did the virus enter the blood? I have told this tale before. I was seven years old, a pupil in my father's Wealden school. Head teachers' sons are never popular, as you may imagine. Yet one day I was invited to join a party of lads to go fishing. First we had to go to the village shop to buy the lines. Each made-up line cost a penny-halfpenny. It was a length of water-cord furnished with a hook, quill float and weight. The rod had to be culled from an ash tree. The line was simply tied on the end. This was as primitive as it got. You could not cast out by more than a few feet into the pond. The bait was a tiny pearl of bread paste seen shining in the depths. You did not watch the float, you concentrated on that white speck and when it disappeared you yanked a tiny roachling out of the water. The silver prize described a parabola through the air to land on the grass behind. The small fish were packed into tins to be taken home for the cats.

That first day, when my white speck vanished, instead of a small fish becoming airborne, the ash plant bowed down to the surface of the water and thrilling electricity ran through it, up my arms and into the very depths of my soul. My excited scream brought my friends around and by a mixture of advice, a huge roach was coaxed up the bank. Both the fish and myself were firmly hooked; me for life.

I can fit that experience into a sort of philosophy, though, for I realised that I was by nature an escapist. I was reared in a world that taught children that they had to face up to reality on their own. Bullying? Fight back no matter the odds; no one will help you. Pains of punishment, dentists or the lancing of boils? The secret was in not caring. Being of my grandfather's race, slight height and build, my answer was to run away, to hide on Guy Fawkes night from the search parties anxious to make me face up to loud bangs. Fishing places, they were the hideaways, the village having a myriad of ponds underneath the stately Bramley apple trees. There could I find peace. It's not exactly a philosophy, is it, to run away from things which frightened me as an under-sized boy ... fireworks, the bone-cracking blows of Punch and Judy shows, and later the air fleets of German bombers which filled the summer skies of 1940, seemingly from horizon to horizon?

Constant fishing brought some expertise, so that when my mother eventually left my father and took me off to Burmarsh, another small village on the Romney Marsh, in 1938 I joined other boys, walking to school across the dykes and sheep pastures to Dymchurch where my eyes were opened. This was a school run by an enlightened headmaster who never hit anyone, never allowed anyone else to hit anyone either. He was light years before his time. There, for the first time, I learned that violence always breeds more violence, solving nothing. My mother was amazed when I brought my school friends home to the converted Victorian railway carriage in which we lived. The Burmarsh lads were giants in comparison to me, but they had a fault. They did not know how to fish. I taught them, and for the first time in my life I became a sort of a hero ... but then came the war and our return to the Wealden village schoolhouse, for my father had been called into the Air Force and later he was sent to South Africa.

What of my 'Fishing Days'? Some years later I had become a pike addict. 'The tyrants of the wat'ry plain' held my dreams in thrall. This was a haunting from the past because in our Wealden village the big pike was spoken of in hushed whispers in the Four Ale Bar. The youngsters were not the only anglers bereft of reels and nets. Pike were also prized for the pot by the families' providers. The flaxen lines, normally tied to the tips of ash plants or bamboo canes, were doubled up. The princely sum of sixpence was spent on a live-bait snap-tackle in the village shop, fearsome treble hooks whipped to gimp. The other prize was the 'bung', the majestic pear-shaped cork float from which to suspend the roach live-bait, duly impaled. The tactic was first to locate the pike. Those farm labourers who worked long hours were not wasting time on prospecting in unrewarding waters. The trick was to find Madame Esox sunning herself in the marginal shallows, and then gently to lower the succulent bait in front of her basilisk eyes. The temptation was too much for the pike; she lanced in fury at the bait. The iron was struck home, and a thrashing of the surface took place, for without the ability to yield line, the great predator had to be held. If she succumbed, then a sheet of newspaper would be lowered down the bank and the fish slid up it, like Clytemnestra of old, to receive her quietus from a rock or branch. It was primitive, but effective.

Now, Mr O. M. A. Reed, a writer with the pen-name of 'Omar', collected records of big pike caught each year in Britain which he published in the *Fishing Gazette*. He had set up a network of informers throughout the land, an intelligence service that would have been admired by spymasters everywhere. I was his 'mole' in Kent.

That cold hand which eventually seizes us all gripped his heart and, knowing his time to be near, he asked his widow-to-be to parcel up his records and send them to me with a request that I compile a book as a memorial to his name. Thus came to light another of my early books, *Big Pike*, perhaps the very first work devoted to the specimens of a single species, and from which the explosive interest of 'specimen hunting' was to dominate angling for decades, giving rise to a rich literature. I was in a quandary, for although the *Angling Times* wanted to publish the book, I was in debt to offer my next manuscript to another publisher, the usual terms of a contract. Then, remembering that dusty manuscript dying of shame in a drawer, I resurrected it and sent it off with little expectation of acceptance. They liked it; the rejection slip never fell through my letter box. And that, my Masters, is how my premature angling autobiography saw the light of day. The contract terms were fulfilled, and *Big Pike* and *Fishing Days* were showered onto an unsuspecting world.

It is bizarre. I fell among pike men though my love was roach, and with seventy-six summers under my belt, nearly every Saturday of the season I am staring at the scarlet tip of a porcupine quill float protruding through the Windsor-soup surface of the River Medway at Tonbridge, still in quest of that mystical three-pound redfin. It must be a truly wild fish, though, dropped into the stream with the palm print of God, for I spurn the new fad of stocked farm ponds where portly roach abound. This is the new habit that coarse fishing has learned from the put-and-take fisheries of the trout angler. Why is it that so many of us yearn for a fair wind for our quarries, unlike the fox hunter's stopped earth, the deer hunter's carted stag, the courser's slipped hare and the trout fisherman's pre-stocked pond?

That is not for me. You may know the tale told by Mr. Skues, of the famous dry-fly man, Mr. Castwell, who, on shuffling off this mortal coil to a better world, was escorted by the Angel to a celestial trout stream. Everything was perfect: a Hardy fly rod, and a box of delectable floating artificial flies, all exact imitations, and a trout rising in a good lie. Mr. Castwell performed the skilful cast; the fish was caught and dispatched. As he was preparing to move off the Angel indicated that another good trout was rising in the self-same lie. He told Mr. Castwell that it was a rigid rule on the fishery that he could not depart in search of another fish as long as one was rising in front of him. So, Mr. Castwell chucked his fly again, nailed the fish ... whereon another one took its place, as the Angel indicated. 'Oh Hell,' Mr. Castwell exclaimed. 'Exactly!' said the Angel. What a helpful ghillie!

Now, if I am to be rewarded similarly for my sins, at least I shall ask to be seated on the lush grass by a secret orchard pond, under a gnarled Bramley tree, in the old Weald, complete with traditional rod – perhaps Spanish Reed? – and a trusty Rapidex centre-pin reel, still my favourite. There are shoals of scintillating roach in front, to one side my evil-smelling rag and ball of bread paste. There should be cooling in the shallows a bottle of that rough cider which they made long ago. To prove it fit to drink you hold it up to the sun. It is no good if you can see through it. It has to be cloudy, with specks of straw and hair from a dead rat, to give it 'body'. 'Oh, Heaven,' I will cry, and hopefully the Angel escort will nod in agreement if I'm in the right place. That will be a benevolent version of *Huis Clos*. Eternity will be bearable. Roach greeted me on my first fishing days. I hope they will be there on my last. Oh, I must keep the Angel off the cider. I can't send him home in that condition, can I?

It was in 1938 when my mother left my father, he of the unspared rod, the authoritarianism of the pre-war Anglican Church, and a roving eye. We had enjoyed our family holidays on the Romney Marsh and this is where she took me, where two-thirds of the landscape is sky, and the dyke-waters are the colour of spent sump oil. I was to discover that the dykes were eel-bound when those sinuous creatures were on the move to the far Sargasso Sea. Only the grey shadow of a mullet investigating the brackish waters stirred the roach-angler's soul.

It is a strange landscape, monotonous in its flatness from the sea to the barrier of the Downs. Its drainage dykes were loved by Bernard Venables, a man I revered. I grew up with his books. I sat next to him at the sunset of his life when he was honoured at a dinner of the Wilton Fly Fishers, and he whispered in my ear, 'I worship words.' And so do I. He would never have been happier than when playing an enormous six-gilled shark in the tropics, but equally content to fish for silver bream in the sewer[1] at Brooklands where the church tower stands in the field beside the church. Cynics say that the tower fell off the church long ago when the first virgin was married there. Optimists reply: 'It will jump back on again when the next one is married there.' Such is Marshland wit.

Each September I lead a party of walkers across the Marsh from Hythe to Dymchurch, to commemorate the fateful Sunday of 3rd September, 1939. Who, of my generation, will forget those words which changed our lives? . . . 'I have to tell you now . . .' They were spoken by another fisherman, Neville Chamberlain, to declare war on Germany. All the villagers of Burmarsh were summoned to a big house where a 'wireless set' was placed on a table in the centre of the lawn. I was missing. I had gone fishing for eels. I was hauled back. No sooner had we heard the speech than far away, wardens were running along the sea wall, blowing whistles to signal the arrival of German bombers. My mother hurried me out on to the marshland where we crouched in a haystack, shivering with fear under the cold, bright sun. It was a false alarm.

---

[1] These are not real sewers but a local name for drainage dykes.

11

In the evening my mother and I strolled down Burmarsh Lane to the old sea wall. The tide was out. Children were scampering about on the sand, but their parents were huddled together in sombre groups. Barely two decades after the end of the Great War memories of the Somme battle still haunted their minds. They knew their lives were about to change. So was mine. My golden days were over.

The beach was crowded. In the afternoon a team of Cossack riders had given a captivating display of their horsemanship. The sand was churned up by the hoof-marks of their mounts.

A young man pushed his way through the crowd. He had two lean greyhounds on leashes. He came up to my mother. He told us that these two hounds were famous on the dog tracks. One of them, Dymchurch Belle, had won many trophies.

'My life is finished. I will be called up for the Army. I have been trying to sell the dogs, but I can't even give them away. They will have to be put down.' He was choking on stifled sobs. The dogs looked up at him, their liquid eyes filled with adoration. My mother loved dogs but she knew our days at Burmarsh were numbered. Sadly she turned away towards the uncaring sea.

At our garden's end was a sluggish dyke. Under our veranda I had fashioned a farm for serpentine lob worms, tea grouts being their favourite diet. Each morning I baited up my set-lines, and at school-day's end I rushed home to recover them to see if an eel had gorged itself. My grandfather, on visit, loved eels, giving his dish the cockney name of 'stoodles' (stewed eels). Yet Mecca for me was the Royal Military Canal which had been excavated along the foot of the Downs to impede the invading army of Napoleon. Here were roach, which I caught with morsels of floating biscuit. When the sun scorched my back at noonday I took my own lunch up the hill to cool my flesh against the ruined walls of Stutfall Castle, a fortress built by the Romans which, according to legend, came to grief as it slid down the hillside. Romans had not learned of watersheds.

When nearly comatose in my bath, I muse that those two years on the Marsh were the sunniest of my boyhood. One day on a Rutulis pilgrimage, I resisted temptation, for crossing the Marsh to Botolphs Bridge on the way to the canal, jumping across a dry ditch, I spied a treasure beyond the dreams of avarice. It was a sumptuous split-cane rod, ready for fishing with a bright, silver centre-pin reel. It had been left in the bottom of the ditch. There was no one in sight. The owner must have been sinking a pint or two in the pub nearby. My fingers itched to take it. Even now I am proud that I did not touch it, my own tackle being cheap and primitive. Even now, when the steam clouds my vision in the bathroom, I feel again that tempting sensation in my fingertips, fingertips I stretched down but regretfully withdrew.

They were two carefree years. My mother was typing away at her novel. I was free from the iron discipline of my father whose religion seemed to have come more from the Old Testament than the New. I absorbed the legends of the Marshmen from my two school friends who were my boon fishing companions. There were the tales of the 'Yellowbellies', Marshmen who, in days gone by, became jaundiced by the Marsh Ague which may have been a form of malaria. Though they changed colour they did not fall very ill themselves. But were a man from Burmarsh to go up the hill to court a girl in Tenterden, and should he bear her home in triumph as a bride, ere long she would sicken and die.

Then there was the legendary smuggling parson of Dymchurch, Dr Syn, whose followers disguised themselves as scarecrows. Did he exist? Go into the church at Snargate. There, on the wall you will read of the great smuggling gangs of yesteryear, 'baccy for the parson and brandy for the squire'. And, yes, they did hide their contraband in the

13

church, so there must have been a priestly confederate. One day someone shopped them. The pony caravan, loaded with baccy and brandy, was ambushed by the Kent militia as it trailed by night across the Marsh. There was a fierce fire-fight in which the Officer in Charge was killed. Many smugglers were caught and no doubt they danced their final hornpipes on the gibbets of Tyburn. Yet a Marshman should die with a smile on his lips; so did he, like the Great Jonathan Wild, take the hangman's gold watch up with him onto the gibbet? How to die laughing? I would fish in the dyke at the bottom of our garden until an evening mist seeped out of the grass to cover the Marsh in ghostly wraiths. When I could no longer see the cork float I had made, I pulled in my line and gazed across the sheep pastures. There, in the mist, would glow the mysterious will-o'-the-wisps, like St Elmo's fire. You could never stalk them, for stretching out my hand to encompass one icy flame, it would immediately disappear. They are said to be made from methane gas in the marsh. I believe they are the souls of dead eel-bobbers and smugglers from long ago.

A strange land, the Romney Marsh, gleaned from the sea, and if predictions of global warming are true, it will return there. Good things come to an end. The poet tells us, 'Dreams without grief are always brief, and once broken, will come not again'.

It is strange that snatches of conversation remain in my mind. I told the lad in the neighbouring school-desk that Paris had fallen. 'Did he hurt himself?' he enquired. Already Authority had decreed that only essential residents would remain in the Marsh. A barrier would be raised along the line of the North Downs. The Marsh would become a foreign country. Those seeking to come and go would have their Identity Cards examined at checkpoints across the narrow lanes. We had to leave with some sixty thousand sheep, the famous Romneys. There I was, squatting at the end of the van which was to take us back to the Weald. My father had been called up for the RAF as he was a member of the Reserve. The new schoolmaster did not need the schoolhouse so the County Education Committee gave us permission to return there. I looked back at that desolate land. Old Nog was the immobile sentinel in the shallows of the dyke. It was my angling competitor. At least I was leaving one efficient angler to snatch eels from the dyke. As the van lurched up the lane towards the hills, on a dead branch of the only tree in that bleak landscape a day-flying owl regarded us solemnly as if to say, 'Goodbye. It's all right for you. You can move away. I have to stay here to find shrews for my ravenous owlets.'

It was believed that the Germans would land on the Marsh. They set up their big guns at Cap Gris Nez. Great fountains of sea-water sprang up as their shells exploded in the harbours at Folkestone and Dover. It was rumoured that Churchill sent a message to Hitler. 'If you come here, there will be no succulent roast lamb for your soldiers. We have taken away all the sheep. Bring your own sausages!' Faced with having to live on that awful German Wurst the Landsers refused to embark, so Hitler sent then to Russia as a punishment. Later, the Grey Men from Whitehall ministries made Marshland shepherds become arable farmers. They cursed Authority as their ploughshares shattered on the iron-hard, buried bog-oaks from the ancient forest of Anderida. When you see the marshland pastures smothered in that sinus-choking yellow rape you have turned a page of history.

Decades later I bumped into the descendants of those evacuated Romney sheep. I was fishing in the Flow Country of Caithness, the best wild brown trout fishing in Europe. The soggy land resembles that of the Rye Marsh where the sheep had grown impervious to foot-rot.

Back in the Weald, I fished for roach in a farm pond. I took time off from float watching to help to usher sheep through a nearby foot-bath of bluestone, the copper-sulphate solution which was later banned.

A relentless teacher in the Weald put my nose to the grindstone to win me a scholarship to Maidstone Grammar School. The only consolation was that like dear old Bernard Venables, I worshipped words and gained there a prize for English. Going up to the platform on Speech Day, I gripped in my grubby hand a pristine copy of Izaak's *Compleat Angler*. And one day, just before we slammed shut the door of our home, that green railway carriage, the postman arrived with the eagerly awaited copy of Allcock's fishing tackle catalogue. I never yearn for 'the gorgeous palaces, nor the cloud-capped towers'. That was a time and place when God was in his Heaven and the old Pullman carriage was Paradise enow. It could not last.

'Never go back,' they say. On my memorial walk this year, I went into the Shepherd and Crook in Burmarsh for a draught of cider. I fell to chatting with a worthy man at the bar. I told him I had once lived in the village. Did he remember our old abode in Donkey Street? 'Can't say,' he replied. 'I come from Lydd, only been here about ten years, so I'm still a stranger and they're not talking to me yet.'

'It was near a dyke-crossing called "Pons Assinorum",' I persisted.

'Oh, nothing like that there now,' he answered. 'There's only that "Donkey Bridge".'

The mournful howl of the miniature locomotive hangs in the air like smoke; it blows away in the wind. The engine is 'Dr Syn'. Its voice is answered by the desolate cry of a curlew across the marsh. A startled heron breaks cover from nearby reed beds, and, croaking in alarm, it melts into the mist. My fellow walkers look bemused, gazing at the desolation. They don't understand my love for the place. 'There are no bloody trees!' one moans at me. Today I stroll with them along Donkey Street. Where once stood our home, 'Burmarsh

View', there is only a scar of burned ground. And, they say, the sea may take back her land to lap against the hillside and the castle wall where bow and stern ropes of Roman ships once were secured to the rusted iron hoops which still remain.

I lean on the gate. Gates in farmland hypnotise me, I hang on them as if drugged. I hallucinate. A gentle sea-fret has rolled across the land. I peer hard into the mist. Time melts away. Three horsemen are shrouded there. 'Where is that traitor, Beckett?' The glint of light on swords and mail fades. They are on their way to Saltmarsh Castle. Then appears through the gloom the pony caravans, loaded with contraband and surrounded by the armed men guarding them in their passage. They, too, are swallowed in the gloaming, on their way to Snargate.

'Stop your dreaming! Are you coming, or what?' shouts one voice. 'Should have been a bloody poet!' sniggers another. I jerk back to reality. No distant musket shots, and the walkers are smiling at me. 'Lunch in the pub, then!' I tell them.

'What do the locals do when this mist comes in like this?' one asks me.

'If you're captain of the cricket team, you win the toss and put the visitors in to bat first,' I tell him.

# 2

*The hop-poles stand in cones,*
*The icy pond lurks under,*
*The pole-tops steeple to the thrones*
*Of stars, sound gulfs of wonder;*
*But not the tallest there, 'tis said,*
*Could fathom to this pond's black bed.*
Edmund Blunden, 'The Midnight Skaters'

'I HAVE TO TELL you now . . .'
Those fateful six words, they did indeed change our lives. Paris fell under the German yoke and their big guns were set up on Cap Gris Nez. We left the Marsh to return to the village in the Weald. My father had been called into the RAF, for he had joined the Volunteer Reserve in 1937, hoping to fly. His age was too much, so they pulled out four of his teeth and trained him in the assembly of Spitfires. Since the new headmaster did not wish to live in the schoolhouse, Authority allowed us to do so.

I discovered a new pond. In the days of railway building they dug ballast holes by the bridges to obtain heavy clay to shore up the banks. These holes eventually filled with water.

Our village had a bridge over the line which ran straight to the channel ports. Some time in the twenties there was a famous actor; his name was renowned. He rose in society but he was embarrassed by his country-girl wife who was semi-literate and whose hard life in the days before his success had eroded the beauty she once had. She had presented him with a daughter. He decided to tuck them away in a remote village where they would be forgotten. The ballast hole had once been converted by some unsuccessful

18

entrepreneur into a lakeside tea-room. Trees were planted to shroud it from the passing trains. Two shanties were erected for accommodation and a flight of steps fell down from the village street to the pond. One would pass by without notice were it not for the creaking signboard.

Time was unkind to the place. Whilst the flappers and their partners whirled away in the Café de Paris in the West End, the famous actor detached his memory from his past. He never saw his wife and child again while he became a household name on stage and radio. As for the tea-room, no one ever came there. No fresh breezes could penetrate the barrier of trees. Everything rotted away. The wooden steps were covered in slime, the decaying tables and chairs, once set in the open for visitors who never arrived, were green with mould. A musty, dank smell pervaded everything, a tang of ooze and decay. The poor woman aged prematurely as if the rot had bitten into her flesh, too. She became a shapeless thing in a filthy apron, ignoring the villagers and being ignored by them. But she had a mysterious pond and a kind heart. I went there, to the shack she shared with her partner, the local chimney sweep. She gave me permission to fish, and also a bar of Sharp's toffee which must have been from the original tea-room stock, but was so soggy as to be impossible to unstick from its wrapping. I trod the landing stage carefully. She had warned me not to venture into the boat; it, too, had crumbled away in the water. The water, though, was not stagnant. It was a clear bottle green, and whilst I gazed into its depths, I saw the silhouette of a tench pass across the shining disc of a white pail top which someone had thrown in.

I told my friend we could fish there. This was in May, 1940, and so secret was the place that we had no need to wait for the opening of the fishing season. Authority would never know we were there. We went to the far end of the pond where it abutted the railway line. We paid no attention to the constant passing of trains, for the traffic was heavy, so heavy that each train had to halt on the far side of the track, opposite to where we were staring at the scarlet tips of our quill floats. Unwittingly, we had stepped into a page of history, for these trains were bearing back to London a defeated army, lifted from the beaches of Dunkirk.

One man did notice. He was a labourer working in the meadow opposite the fishing place. Being curious, he went up to the wire fence. As a train stopped, the carriage windows were lowered, and an odd soldier even opened a door to go down onto the carriage step. They told him of Dunkirk, of evacuation, and perhaps he asked, perhaps he did not, but his ears were saluted with the impedimenta of war. He staggered home laden with an army greatcoat, a jack knife, a few tins of emergency rations. That night, in the bar of the Prince of Wales he displayed his booty, told his tale. Next day there was a group of villagers hanging on the wire, holding out their arms in supplication. Day by day the crowd grew larger, surrounding villages furnished their congregations to the new cargo religion. Naturally, we deserted our rods to join the throng.

The village policeman ran up and down the wire in desperation. At first he tried to prevent the Manna from Heaven, but in the end he knew he could not cope. He reached an agreement with the beggars, that if they handed in actual weapons, rifles and bayonets, they could keep the rest. This is a tale which has never been told. In the cinema newsreels in Maidstone, and in the daily papers, displayed there were the pictures of grinning soldiers at Dover, mugs of tea and doorstep sandwiches in hand, the cheerful, undaunted British Tommies. In fact it was a defeated, demoralised army jettisoning its equipment and telling those who asked that the German army would be in Kent in a fortnight.

Fifty years later, unexpectedly my wife asked me to drive her to 'my village'. I had never been back. I told her that no one would remember the puny schoolmaster's son who went fishing. Rural communities had burned away in the fire of progress. Machines had replaced men. Tied cottages were snapped up by commuters. Even so, when we went into the church some ladies were parcelling up fruit for the old folk, and on my introducing myself, one of them replied that she remembered me well as, when she was five, I had recruited her to dig for moles in a nearby field. She recollected that she had joined the throng of hunters, but being too small to win a trophy, she had burst into tears.

I, too, was small and slower at beating the horny hands of farm workers to rifle the meadow grass for prizes. I had one ace-in-the-hole, a recollection of some rudimentary French from my great uncle. So, when a *poilu* emerged from the carriage to the step, I asked him, '*Qu'est-ce que se passe?*', to which he replied, '*Nous sommes foutus*', going on to give me the usual message that the Boches were on his heels. He presented me his helmet, with the grenade image on the front, an army water bottle and a scented prayer book with enamelled picture of Virgin and Child on the cover. I must have felt guilty, for later I gave them up to raise money for the village Spitfire fund.

The trains ran on for many days, some bearing huge red crosses and filled with soldiers in the bright-blue uniforms and red ties of the wounded. When these hospital trains stopped there, the begging tongues fell silent.

Gradually peace returned to the line. We returned to the fishing, without, perhaps, realising that we had seen history in the making. And we went back to the hidden pond, climbing cautiously down the rickety staircase, under the rusting sign which still bore the optimistic words from the piping days of peace, 'Bridge Lake Tea Rooms'. Perhaps, too, it did impinge on my young consciousness that a brooding pessimism had entered the community. Everyone was fearful as to what was to come. The ten-acre fields were studded with upright balks of timber to smash up gliders.

Old soldiers, survivors from the bloody fields of the Somme, formed a section of the Home Guard, at first known as the Local Defence Volunteers (LDV). The village bobby called to remove the distributor from the car my father had stored away for the duration. It was for adults a time of foreboding, brought home to me by blacked-out windows by night, criss-crossed with strips of sticky brown paper by day. I suppose I lacked the imagination of those who talked with darkened tones in the bar-rooms. What did I do? I went fishing, escaping again. I was not the only one, for years later I read a book by H. E. Bates, *The Country Heart*. He was living in the Weald at that time. Nearby was a section of soldiers, perhaps manning guns or searchlights, or waiting in trepidation for the clamour of church bells announcing the invasion. Of an evening he invited the soldiers to fish his pond. Their sergeant moodily stared at the electric-blue flash of a kingfisher, unconcernedly going about the business of feeding its family, and he said: 'If it weren't for the fishing, we'd all go bloody mad.'

# 3

*What is this, the sound and rumour?*
*What is this that all men hear,*
*Like the wind in hollow valleys*
*When the storm is drawing near,*
*Like the rolling on of ocean*
*In the eventide of fear?*

William Morris

I CONJURE UP OUR village as it was when we returned there from the Romney Marsh in 1940. I remind you of the stream that ran nearby, a stream with two dead poets, one at each end. There was my favourite, Edmund Blunden, whose father was the schoolmaster at Yalding. Perhaps Yalding's most famous son; a verse of his is engraved on a window in the church there. The other was Siegfried Sassoon. Both were anglers, for Blunden's account of the Miller being startled by the swirl of a great pike in the mill pool came from an acquaintance with fish. Then Sassoon fished the Teise where it wended its way through the golf course at Lamberhurst. I have oft lazed on the bridge in the village street to marvel at the lithe trout on the tobacco-stained stones below, for the river has the tinge of the Iron Masters of old. Both poets were warriors on the Somme battlefield, both earning their Military Crosses there. Sassoon was to toss his medal into the Mersey; the blood-price of battle was telling on his mind.

Sassoon hunted these fields with Weldishmen before that bloody conflict. He survived the war, village legend having it that he batted with a good eye into his seventies but, being too arthritic to bend, he stopped the ball with his ankles, whilst fielding at deep cover ... ouch! He described his fox-hunting life in *Memoirs of a Fox-hunting Man*. He had a hell of a problem tying his stock. He disguised the names of places and people, and admirers like myself enjoyed puzzling out the truths. I shall not disguise the name of my village, I shall simply omit it. You may puzzle it out yourself, for I cycled three miles to Yalding for a haircut and two miles to have a tooth pulled in Marden.

There was a mystery about the village. The tied cottages were strung along a street. Halfway through the village another road came in at a right angle, the Marden road, and here stood the school, the schoolhouse and the church. Nearby was an old manor house of Tudor times. That was bizarre for there were no other dwellings of a similar age. I guessed that a former hamlet had been wiped out by plague. Then, when hops and apples revived the Weald after the iron makers emigrated to the more efficient coal-firing of the North, the clearance of the Anderida Forest had revealed a bare clay soil which was kind to the brewers and fruit farmers. A 'modern' village grew up, surrounded by orchards and hop gardens.

Perhaps the 'Garden of England' was really a hop garden. Why should hops grow in gardens rather than fields? The legend is that an Archbishop of Canterbury levied a tax on fields. Farmers responded by saying, 'Ah, we don't grow hops in fields, we grow them in gardens.' There are other legends about hops. Walton tells us that 'hops, carps, turkeys and beer came into England in the same year'.

Employers had a problem. Their labourers were swilling so much beer that they snoozed under the noonday sun. The answer was to make the beer so bitter that they would not drink so much. They turned to a parasitic plant called 'Lupus', the 'wolf of the willow'. It strangled trees. They found that they could grow it up strings tied to the tops of tall poles. They created their own vocabulary. The earth-mounds below the poles for the plants were called 'hills'. The best, cheap fertiliser was shoddy from the clothing trade, dug into the hills. This practice was known as nidgeting. The strings and supporting wires were fixed to the tops of poles by 'stiltmen'. A drunken Yorkshireman once swung a punch at me for telling him about the stiltmen, but it wasn't even 1st of April. The bitter taste of hops became popular. Just as Greeks add resin to bottled wine to replicate the taste of the wineskins of old, so did the beer-quaffers demand hops for their beer, and thus was born the 'bitter ale'. We drink it till we die.

The first time I flew over the Weald I gazed down on the orchards and hop gardens where a myriad of points of light reflected the sun's rays. These were the secret ponds. They had been dug by Huguenot refugees expelled from France by the Sun King, Louis XIV. They were weavers. They settled in the Weald to make the Kentish broadcloth and they needed to impound water. Thus, years later into my City shop came Judge Rougier who told me that his ancestors settled there and took their family name from the dyeing red of the cloth, and perhaps their fuller's pond became one of my roach haunts, who knows? It was said that myriads of such fisheries were made by the Huguenots.

Behind our schoolhouse were orchards. The farm belonged to 'Hopper' Levett, one-time wicket keeper for Kent and England, who, alas, due to his incompetence with the bat, ceded his England place to Les Ames. Did he keep wicket for our village team? The only tale that came down to me was that in a needle match we bowled out Yalding for three runs, then went on to lose the match with a miserly score of two. My father, the team's demon fast bowler, told me that the pitch was like the Himalayas; he would have liked to fold it up, put it into his cricket bag and take it with him everywhere.

Hopper's eye was keen. He spurned the usual net when the ferret was put down the rabbit hole. He never missed

25

the bolting bunny. I asked his permission to fish the ponds in his orchards. This was readily given, save for Sundays. It was to one of these ponds I ran, under the majestic Bramley apple trees which are now vanishing from the Weald in favour of the stunted dwarfs which are replacing them. The first action was to shin up a tree overhanging the water, to locate the shoals of roach.

There was the fateful Sunday in August. The village folk were dispersing from the morning service. It was a dog day, sultry with the hops hanging heavily on the bines, unmoved by even the ghost of a breeze. People were leaving on foot, on bikes, to return for the Sunday roast. My mother lingered to speak to the Vicar in the street. A farm worker stood nearby gazing at the sky towards the east. There seemed to be uneasiness in the air despite the windless noon. The sky above was a clear vault of cobalt, cloudless. 'Seems to be thunder, a long way off,' he said. True, there was a faint rumbling to the east. A summer storm, perhaps?

The rumbling was continuous. My mother and the Vicar paused in their conversation. The Vicar seemed to be perturbed. 'That doesn't sound like thunder,' he said. And then a flight of three Spitfires passed overhead, climbing upwards from their base at West Malling and tearing the air like calico. 'I think the bombers are coming,' he added. We craned our necks, staring over the tops of the hop-poles towards the east, whilst remaining silent.

The distant noise increased. From out of the continuous rumour came occasional staccato bursts of sound, now unmistakably distinct as the engines of aircraft. The air fleet arrived at great height like tiny silver fish in a clear, deep-blue sea.

When describing that day in after-life I was often told, 'It must have been exciting for you.' To the watchers on the ground the battle was at tremendous height. It was impossible to tell friend from foe as the smaller fighter planes weaved mysteries of smoke in and out of the armada.

The battle did pass directly over our village and died away to the west. At its height there was a roar of the bombers' engines overlaid by the occasional howl of a diving fighter plane, and the threnody of machine-gun fire. Yet, in a way we felt detached. True, it was awe inspiring and the weight of the attack filled us with pessimism, for we feared the invasion would follow, that nothing could stop this great air fleet. And it came on successive days, duly at noon as if on a timetable, so that knots of watchers gathered in the street, for the Marden road, running directly to the east, opened our eyes to a low horizon.

Regularly the battles faded away westwards and the sky was at peace save for the sounds of full summer, bees foraging in the golden hops, a man starting up a tractor in the farmyard, a child laughing in the Vicarage garden. Strangely, too, the planes dispersed and none reappeared so that I was allowed to collect my rod and cross the orchard to the roach pond. As someone said of war, there are long periods of boredom with acute interludes of sheer terror. Strange, too, we became used to it. Field workers would glance upwards from time to time, then bend again to their work. Then, as if listening to the football results, wireless sets would be tuned in to the evening news to be cheered by the exaggerated claims of Fighter Command.

It was not to remain like that.

That day the battle had passed. In late afternoon I was summoned to the torture of a piano lesson by the lady-organist of the church. I found it hard to read music, I was too lazy to practise but she needed the weekly ten-bob note from my mother. I was fumbling with the keys whilst Miss Foreman's eyes glinted with exasperation through her pince-nez. The agony was relieved by the appalling cacophony of a bellowing engine almost over the roof-top, and the overpowering scream of eight machine guns. Rushing out into the school-yard we saw a Dornier, the elegant silhouette we called a

'Flying Pencil', thundering overhead with a Hurricane fighter glued to its tail. Yellow smoke was pouring from the stricken plane as it dived to earth some half-mile away.

The word was passed round that the village folk could visit the scene of the crash after eight o'clock in the evening, when the official wreckage inspectors had finished their work. We gathered in a procession by the church for the 'off'. The Dornier had crashed into a hop garden. The taut wires between the poles had shredded it on impact, scattering the remains over many square yards. The tale was told of a farm worker ploughing between the 'hills' on which the hops grew when the plane struck near him. The crew were killed by gunfire and the tearing wires, save miraculously one man who, staggering from the debris, covered in blood, went towards the tractor. The labourer, seeing this ghastly apparition approaching, and his ears stunned by the horrendous noise, jumped from his seat and ran for dear life whilst the tractor, unmanned, continued an erratic course until it buried itself in the grassy bank of the River Teise. The first on the scene were worthy men of Dad's Army, having rushed home from the fields to don their uniforms.

By the time we arrived the bodies had been removed. There I saw my first signs of human mortality. The bucket seat of the pilot was pepper-potted with bullet holes and it had been drenched with blood, which was now drying to a rusty-brown colour as the evening sun percolated through the hop-bines. Perhaps I lacked imagination in my eleventh year. It was years later that I pictured four young men, excited and perhaps a little frightened, climbing into that slim, beautifully shaped bomber on another field in France. Of all the bombers we saw that year, the Dornier was the most handsome. We cannot remember the future, time does not flow in that direction, and for those young men, they could not have known that they were flying to their Doomsday . . .

28

I was sickened by the scene. Did the spilt blood smell? I know not. I walked up the field to the bank of the Teise.

The evening sun shone into the water, illuminating one of those gilded pools which chuckled down into a typical 'run'. A shoal of chub was lying there, the grey shadows in formation, small ones to the front, large ones to the rear. I had not yet fished the river; I was in my 'farm pond period'. I did not realise then that this stream would play such a life-forming role, teaching me how to put a dry-fly with pin-point accuracy to a rising trout, or to push my rod through a bush to drop a live mayfly to tempt a chub loafing in a quiet pool. Yes, the stream would be my schoolroom and my delight, but that life was still to come.

That summer of 1940 passed with a dreamlike quality. The first bombers came before the annual invasion of hop-pickers from the East End of London. They arrived in high summer. In the piping days of peace this would have been a holiday for them, returning home, the parents with money, the children with the 'hopper's apple' traditionally to be given to the teacher when school started. This autumn many would have returned to shattered homes in Dockland. My father, on leave, insisted that his son should 'see history', and drove through the bombed streets where I was left with the indelible memory of a bath hanging from its pipes from the sheer upper wall of a devastated house. On glancing back through the pages of *Fishing Days*, I noted that the fly-leaf blurb described me as 'escaping the Battle of Britain, fishing rod in hand'.

Happily, the other memories are there, the golden days by the pond, under the apple trees, alone as an angler should be. It is imperative that the tip of the float must be scarlet to have that mesmerising effect. The colour of the water is clear sepia. I can see the tiny white pearl of paste in the depths and the roachlings fuss about it. In the bay an eel is buried in the mud but its head protrudes. It is on the watch. A young jack-pike is sunbathing before the reeds; his green and yellow flanks reflect the light, giving him away to my eyes. A kingfisher makes that electric-blue flash over the dusty-still surface of the pond. All is at peace; all is as it should be. There could be no better place on earth. Here, I forgot Authority, and for a while, Authority forgot me. I would put out of my mind tomorrow morning, the scrubbing in cold water at the stone kitchen sink, the smell and sting of carbolic soap, the hours of parental watchfulness till the bombers come.

And then to scamper to the pond in the peace of the afternoon; roach-fever, a blood infection which lasts for life and for which there is no cure. Escape? Of course!

# 4

*He on the sandbank lies,*
*Sunning himself long hours*
*With stony gorgon eyes:*
*Westward the sun lowers.*
*Sudden the gray pike changes, and quivering poises for*
*    slaughter;*
*Intense terror wakens around him; the shoals scud awry,*
*    but there chances*
*A chub unsuspecting; the prowling fins quicken, in fury he*
*    lances;*
*And the miller that opens the hatch stands amazed at the*
*    whirl in the water.*

Edmund Blunden, 'The Pike'

I THINK I KNOW that spot well. Blunden must have strolled out from Yalding along the road to Hunton village where the River Beult loops in towards the lane. There once stood the mill. I, too, passed that way down to the river, later in the war when Authority placed two bombed-out families in the wing of the Tudor manor at Buston. My mother and I, we were refugees from the wreckage of our house in suburbia, now coming back to the Weald. I was still somewhat fearful of that supreme killing machine, the pike, whose prey could never escape once the needle teeth took hold, for they sloped backwards on hinges to give the miserable victim a one-way ticket to the dining room – but not as a guest! I recall the words of the French entomologist, Fabre, 'the Intestine rules the World'.

I was still besotted with roach and pike fever did not gain hold of me until the fifties when 'Omar' recruited me as his successor. It was then that I fell amongst pike-men. They were a strange race, carved from teak their weather-worn faces, and their eyes were faded to light grey as they passed hours surveying the February chill of Hickling Broad and Horsey Mere where the great predators lived. Such a man I came to know and respect: Edwin, son of the famed Jim Vincent. Pike anglers paused when you mentioned Jim's name. A light came into their eyes. 'Ah,' said one such man to me, 'in the war there were only two heroes here, Churchill and Jim Vincent . . . not necessarily in that order.' Jim had joined the Ages before I arrived at the Pleasure Boat Inn at Hickling, for in those days this was the Mecca for pike men. I already knew Edwin by reputation because I had written to him when completing the records bequeathed to me by Omar.

I do not know why Edwin took me under his wing, but a man cannot live without honour, and I felt honoured to be accepted so young. I was also unskilled in casting dead baits from the Ariel centre-pin reels, an art long forgotten today. This was the only method Edwin used, the knowledge handed down from father to son. It was simple and deadly. A small dead roach was threaded up with a wire trace from vent to snout and a huge treble hook snuggled into the vent to act as a keel. In the water the bait lurched about like a drunken sailor; the pike could not resist. Edwin had made some tremendous hauls on Horsey Mere, one catch being surmounted by a monstrous old harridan of over thirty pounds, for the biggest pike are all ladies, the sort you would want to slip into your landlady's bath. Edwin was a master of his father's craft. Every winter I came to Hickling to share his boat and his knowledge.

Pike lore isn't just about the fish. It is also about the pike-men and their lives. Thus it was that Edwin told me that when his father was dying he gave instructions for the disposal of his ashes. Edwin was to take the urn afloat on the Broad and spread them on the water when the first pike came to the gaff. A baby eleven-pounder succumbed to temptation by Pleasure Boat Island and Jim went to join the race of *Esox* which he had nurtured over the years, mixing the blood line of the native fish with lovers from other waters. Inbreeding is weakening for both fish and humans, you see.

Sadly, Edwin had the task of taking the ashes of his mother to the same spot just some months later.

He told me a tale of a man who wrote to him after the war. This man had never fished for pike. He became a prisoner of war in the hands of the Japanese but, although savagely treated and starved, he survived, though in very poor health. For some reasons which we could not fathom, in captivity he dreamed of catching a great pike on Hickling Broad. He wanted to survive to do that. He knew of the Vincent fame and asked Edwin to take him out. Edwin obliged, though he was dismayed at the poor man's pitiable appearance. The two of them went afloat, the mud anchor was lowered and Edwin worked the boat down wind. Then the man's rod bent into a good fish which he brought to the gaff. Whilst Edwin brought the fish aboard he saw that his guest was wracked with sobs; streaming down his thin cheeks were floods of tears. Edwin himself was too choked to speak. And not long after he learned that the man had died.

Too many years later, when Bernard Venables and I had several decades under our belts I asked him about his experiences with Jim Vincent and Edwin. Bernard had already described[1] how Jim had lost the fish of a lifetime. How much would it have weighed? Thirty pounds? Forty pounds? It was a Grendel-like monster, as the one Beowulf slew in an enchanted mere. It fell to Jim's companion to gaff the fish. In those days the gaff was slipped through the lower jaw of the pike by an expert's hand, the target being much like that tiny area where the skilled matador has to plunge his sword

---

[1] Bernard Venables, *A Fisherman's Testament*, 1949, Medlar edition 1997.

between the shoulder-blades of a Miura bull. A miss would be disaster for both men. And Jim's friend missed his stroke, breaking the trace. The fish of a lifetime sank down into the bitter water of Hickling. Jim said not a word; what could he have said? The two men remained good friends for ever, and Bernard rightly refused to reveal the name of the man whose flawed stroke set free the great fish.

Bernard could cap this sad story. One day there appeared a notice on the village hall at Hickling that Jim Vincent would give a talk on how to catch a big pike. A rather sadistic wag added the words, 'And So-and-so will tell you how to lose it'.

Bernard loved to go afloat with Edwin on the delightfully lily-padded Lady Broad in the Ormesby Group. Bernard, though, adored the clockwork-engined multiplying reels of which he was a master. He popped his gaily coloured plugs between the lilies for summer pike. I was invited to stay there by the master of documentary films, Harold White. Of an evening we would play with his fabulous model-train layout, based perhaps on his *Flying Scotsman* film. Of a morning I would push out in his small boat, and paddling into the secret Lady Broad, I thought of the days when Bernard and Edwin were gazing into the bottle-green water for the terrifying viragos, those gorgon-eyed pike which patrolled the bream shoals. Hampton, in his gloriously illustrated book on pike, likened them to the guardians of a police state which swooped down on the unfortunate individualist.

Not all men of Norfolk are obsessed with pike, but the local parson was. It seems that a lady came to the church to book a christening for the following Tuesday, but the Sexton told her this was impossible. It would have to be Thursday.

'But why the delay?' enquired the frustrated mother.

'You see, ma'am, Wednesday is the Vicar's pike-fishing day and he keeps the live bait in the font.'

Fishermen, you understand, do have a proper sense of priorities.

When I wrote *Fishing Days* long ago, I looked at the fishing scene through rose-tinted lenses. I want this one to be a sunny book, too, for ours is a happy sport. There were sometimes shadows on the water. The first shadow was, perhaps, when Omar's pike records came to me and I noticed that the name of a renowned pike fisherman was never given. If you investigate pike records you cannot help but discover examples of the exaggeration of the size and weight of 'big fish'. There is something about the pike which excites even the non-angling public, and reputations are made in the media. Long ago, such false claims were exposed; then genuine pike men become incandescent, understandably so. The trouble is that a twenty-pound pike is so impressive it is possible to let it grow a few extra pounds after death. It has been known for a cheat to stretch a fish to make it worthier on the Mona scale. The tragedy is that on rare occasions a good angler can become the prisoner of his own reputation, especially if he claims he can 'catch pike to order'.

It goes without saying that during my career as a pike ferret I came across many fraudulent claims. One of the strangest was unmasked by another writer with a keen eye and a twitching nose. This was Brian Harris, the editor of a popular magazine, *Angling*. I cannot recollect the name of the perpetrator of this rather clever deception. He got hold of a reasonably impressive double-figure pike. To convert it to an even more enviable size he broke the spine of the fish and simply stretched it to match the claim on the Mona scale. Then the fish was mummified by a taxidermist. The illusion was expertly contrived. It seems there was a commercial motive, given the astronomical prices paid by fanatical collectors for embalmed fish-corpses entombed behind glass.

So whilst ferreting out fraudulent claims I must confess that there are two sides to this coin. What is *even* more irritating is when a genuine claim is rejected by rumour and innuendo. I write with feeling. It happened to me.

I describe elsewhere that some years ago the lower reaches of the Medway were so polluted that like her sister, the Thames, that river would not allow migratory fish to win through to the higher spawning grounds. Some sea trout were seen to congregate at the Allington locks, but they could not surpass the barrage of lock-gates and weirs. No salmon, no sea trout had been caught over many decades in the Upper Medway.

There dawned one of those magically sunny February days. It tempted me to swim a few maggots for roach above Tonbridge at a place called Six Arches where an island divides the current. The flow was fining down after a rain deluge. Reacting to a firm bite, to my amazement I caught a sea trout of some three pounds, a fresh-run silver peal in magnificent condition. As it was out-of-season I returned it carefully to the stream.

Shortly afterwards my float obligingly submerged. This capture was a carbon copy of the first, with one exception. A monstrous sea-fisherman's hook, trailing a length of thick nylon, was embedded deeply in the fish's gullet. I had no option other than to kill the poor pilgrim, reflecting that at least none could deny my unusual exploit.

I took the fish to the local tackle shop in Tonbridge where the proprietor photographed it for me. Then I deposited it in the deep freeze at the cottage of a nearby friend and reputable angler, Richard Briggs. We left a message in the shop that we would keep the fish for two weeks in case any official wished to confirm its identity. By its appearance there could be no doubt. No one bothered to call.

Understandably, some club officials were concerned that if the Upper Medway gained the reputation of becoming a salmon and sea-trout river, either their rents would be raised dramatically by riparian owners or those landlords would replace their coarse fishing clubs with syndicates of affluent game-fishermen. This is no joke. I fear it is already happening in Teesdale where considerable runs of salmon have appeared after decades of estuarine pollution. The once-toxic flow from factories was clarified by the Thatcher policy of de-industrialisation of the North-East. Migratory fish returned.

There is a tragic end to this story. I had a friend who was an addict to drowning lug worms from the end of Southend Pier. For two years or so he had suffered with back pains which were diagnosed as a slipped disc until the pain was so agonising that they put him through the tunnel of a body scanner. He had an inoperable tumour of the pancreas. The hospital sent him home to die. I took the fish to his home. It was gorgeous to eat. A few weeks later he died, though in his early fifties. His wife, Katherine, was a gifted musician who, years before, had met her husband Peter as both were members of the National Youth Orchestra. She collected the remainder of his drugs. She hid herself so effectively in the local woodland that her body was not found for nine days. A memorial seat to Katherine was placed to overlook a small pool and the butterfly house.

Whilst carp fishing became the saving grace for coarse fishermen, fly fishing competitions brought an unhealthy commercialism into our sport. To me it was the antithesis of the spirit of fly fishing. Eventually it even invaded the River Test where each competitor was accompanied by an official for the day. A keeper I knew was asked by his celebrated fisherman to accept a trout or two which were millimetres below the size limit. The keeper declined.

'Other people are doing it,' protested the would-be cheat.

'I'm sorry, Sir. You've got the wrong man.'

It was not unknown for a trout slightly shorter than the size limit to have its spine broken before being stretched to the acceptable length.

I was amused on seeing the weigh-in after a match on Lough Conn. The trout were hung head-down on a wooden scaffold. A well-known competitor hung up a beautiful orange trout, much bigger than those of his rivals. Its mouth was agape. Suddenly a bright stream of snails shot out of its maw on to the ground, losing about a pound of its weight.

In some lakes a minority of trout take up a specialised feeding habit. In Blagdon they gorge on Corixa. In many deep lakes and lochs where the normal trout stock is somewhat stunted some trout develop a cannibalism habit. They can grow to an immense size. They are called 'Ferox'. Although some experts claim them to be a separate subspecies of brown trout with their own particular DNA pattern, the monsters which were caught in the Queen Mary reservoir in London were survivors of the original stocking of fingerling brown trout. It is possible that there are two distinct races of Ferox trout, one being normal brown trout which grow on from the native stock, the other being a separate race of fish particular to deep lochs in Scotland. This is a controversy which so far has no conclusion. The few Ferox I have seen and the one I caught in Cow Green were all beautiful fish, contrary to the legend that Ferox were ugly, ill-conditioned brutes with jaws like a bull terrier's.

In alkaline lakes some trout crunch water snails. I have caught such fish. Surprisingly, they are lethargic in their fight when hooked. They have thicker stomach walls to cope with digesting hard shells.

The snail-eaters in Lough Conn become orange in colour. I was delighted that Authority did not allow this angler to scoop up the regurgitated snails to thrust them back into the trout's gullet.

As I sit here to write, I see again the staithe at Hickling.

Edwin is waiting for me whilst he chats to George Gibson, the warden, whose golden Labrador, Sandy, waits patiently nearby. The air from Siberia sweeps across the water, reminding me of those words of John Masefield ... *the wind's like a whetted knife* ... and whilst the two men are completely impervious to it, I feel as if the flesh is being flayed from my bones. I know I have to go out with Edwin as I have passed myself off as a pike-man. We are going up to Dead-man's Hole, so called because a murderer put the corpse of his victim under a raft of floating vegetation. I have mastered the Aerial reel. I can send out a quarter-pound dead roach and wobble it back through the shallow water. I blink through a flurry of snow flakes. There is a swirl. I have hooked a modest jack-pike. Then, immediately the old ten-footer of split cane bows down to the water god as a big pike seizes the smaller jack across its flanks. There is no chance of landing it. There is no hook in its mouth. We have a glimpse of that vast flank, flecked with emeralds and gold, a pair of jaws clamped like a vice on its dinner and two gun-barrel eyes staring at us. Then nothing save a well-lacerated two-pounder twitching on the surface ... 'maybe your first thirty?' says Edwin. Maybe, maybe not. For as old Izaak told his pupil who bemoaned a lost chub ... 'take note, no one can lose that which he never had'.

It was a sad day when John Burret arrived at my front door bearing a capacious cardboard box. This was Omar's archive of records of large pike caught each year in the British Isles. In addition to the book he wanted me to write, he also bequeathed to me his work of collating pike records for his annual big pike list in the *Fishing Gazette*. My own fishing hero was Bernard Venables. I admired his philosophy of fishing anywhere for anything. It was with some reluctance that I became a single-species hunter between October and March during the nineteen-sixties.

Becoming a pike ferret for the *Fishing Gazette* changed

my life, at least for the remaining years of that magazine.

I did not realise at the time that I would become Omar's successor. The phone rang by day, by night. Sheaves of letters tumbled through my door. Countless invitations arrived for me to join expeditions with famous anglers, even though I had to earn my daily bread in the laboratory.

Omar had established his own ground rules for the claiming of a true specimen pike. Although specimen hunting was then in its infancy, clearly it would become a dominant philosophy in our sport. It could be foreseen that clubs would be formed, dedicated to the captures of single species such as pike and carp. These rules became standard procedures in all record-listing organisations in angling. It was already apparent that specimen hunting would be linked to the reputations of celebrated fishermen. Income and prize money would now enter angling in a big way.

What were these rules? Firstly, the fish had to be weighed on recognised scales. These scales would need to be authenticated by testing. Two witnesses were required to weigh the fish or to have seen it weighed. One of these witnesses would have to be completely independent, for obviously the captor would be fishing with a friend who might be too supportive. This became a controversy on occasion, for the companion's own reputation might also be reflected by the image of the celebrity with whom he was fishing. For this reason the testimony of a completely independent witness was paramount. This would interdict scepticism by envious competitors. It explains why Richard Walker presented his record carp, Clarissa, to the London Zoo's aquarium. I was one angler who made the pilgrimage to see that living oracle.

These basic rules would need to be applied rigorously because of the British custom of returning coarse fish to the water. Omar would not accept any claim which did not conform to these criteria. To avoid unpleasant controversy he would simply omit the dubious claim from his record list.

He did discuss some historic big-pike claims where he thought an error had been made in recording their weights. I decided to follow his precepts.

I had noted that Omar did not record the claims of the celebrated Norfolk pike angler, Dennis Pye. On enquiry, I was told by John Burret that Omar had been unable to authenticate some of Pye's claims. His 'moles' in Norfolk were dubious about them. To convey some of the stress involved in rejecting a big pike claim, I describe the case of the claim made by Dennis Pye for the capture of a 34 lb 2 oz pike in Horsey Mere in March 1965. Horsey Mere, in Norfolk, was renowned for being the home of gigantic *Esox*. A local angler with whom I fished, Len Spencer, had a properly authenticated 34 lb pike to his credit. I mention this to confirm that Spencer, a professional photographer by trade, knew what a fish of that size would look like.

Pye did not make his claim to me. It was his purpose to enter the capture for the prestigious prize offered each season by a regional newspaper. Horsey Mere opened for coarse fishing only for the last few days of each season. Alas, I was never able to take a fishing holiday at that time. It was also necessary to go afloat to cover the haunts of the big predators.

Live-baiting was not allowed. Pye caught his fish on a dead-bait. Needing an independent witness, he spotted Edwin Vincent fishing with Len Spencer. He knew that Vincent was the son of the famous Broadland warden, Jim Vincent. Like his father, Edwin was known locally as a man of integrity. Recognising that Edwin would be an ideal independent witness, he punted across to his boat and asked him to sign the claim-document he had already prepared. Edwin had caught a prodigious number of big pike up to 31 lb. Like his father, he would recognise by sight a 30 lb-plus pike.

Edwin was in an emotional state when he phoned me. He confessed that he had made the biggest mistake of his life.

Edwin and Len Spencer joined Pye and his companion on the bank by the Summer House. Edwin could see a big pike lying in Pye's boat.

Unfortunately, being a trusting soul, Edwin signed the paper which Pye had prepared, but without first weighing the fish. However, whilst Pye was fiddling with his document Edwin took a close look at the pike. This fish did not appear to be anything like 34 lb. Its girth was neither deep nor firm enough, as confirmed by the photograph Spencer took. Edwin scooped up the pike and weighed it on his own Salter spring balance. Immediately he protested to Pye that the fish weighed only 24 lb. Pye told Edwin that he had weighed the fish twice on different scales so Edwin's balance must be faulty.

When Edwin returned home he checked his spring balance with fruit-weights he kept for his daily work. His balance read true.

He asked me if he should withdraw his witness statement. I advised him not to do so as he would be accused of envy of Pye. He implored me not to write about the incident during his lifetime. He was ashamed at having been duped. I promised, though he allowed me one exception. My book, *Big Pike*, was being processed by Peter Tombleson for the *Angling Times* collection. Tombleson noticed that I did not record any of Pye's claims. I related the incident to him. He agreed that the photograph of the fish did not appear to be consistent with the claimed weight. He also had some dubiety about previous claims by Pye.

Years passed. Edwin and Dennis Pye had died. I was no longer bound by my promise to Edwin. I discussed the incident with John Watson, editor of *Pikelines*, the house magazine of the Pike Anglers Club. He persuaded me to write about this experience for his members. The article appeared in their magazine in 1983. With the passing years my own pike fever had abated. My reputation in angling was rooted in fly fishing.

Since the evidence was overwhelming that Pye had exaggerated the weight of this pike by about 10 lb, I was astonished when in 2011 I learned that my account of this event was being denied by Pye's companion on that fateful day. He questioned Vincent's account of weighing the fish at 24 lb. He told us that the fish was weighed at 34 lb in the boat before he came ashore with Pye to meet Edwin. Remember, *Edwin had not seen the fish being weighed in Pye's boat*. He went on to say that Edwin did not weigh the fish at all. He did not realise the consequences of his statement, which, if true, would have meant that Pye had submitted an invalid claim signed by an independent witness who had not authenticated the weight of the capture, nor seen it weighed by its captor. Any recording committee would have thrown out such a claim and disqualified it. He did not realise that unwittingly he made his own case that Pye's claim was fraudulent. No one would accept a claim when the independent witness had neither seen the fish weighed nor weighed it himself. Significantly, no measurement was given to check on the Mona scale.

I had no personal axe to grind. My approach to this event was the same as it was for every claim which was made by those who wished to enter a capture for the annual list of big pike. Undoubtedly Pye's claim was questionable. Yet I was bound by the promise I made to Edwin not to write about it during his lifetime. I kept my word even though Colin Dyson wrote in *Pikelines* that the story was well known in Norfolk years before.

Not long after the original event the Thurne system was invaded in the late sixties by a toxic substance called Prymnesium. It killed fish over miles of river and lake.

Dennis Pye was put on the back-burner by the angling press. Angling is a sport of fashion. Being curious about this I enquired with professionals. They told me that as Pye was no great shakes as a pen-man he had agreed that an EMAP journalist, Peter Collins, should handle all his publicity. Collins ghost-wrote Pye's book. As his fame grew Pye was sought by television directors and the national press. He was persuaded he could earn more by going direct to the media. Collins was not too pleased; nor was the *Angling Times*.

But carp fever was taking over. Other writers were taking a longer look at Pye's reputation. The growing philosophy of specimen hunting demanded a less casual way of 'guestimating' the weight of fish. They discovered other examples of exaggeration in Pye's claims. I select only one of many expressions of doubt collated by Graham Booth in an exhaustive inquiry in *Pikelines 26*. I quote from an article written by the angling writer Colin Dyson. Dyson fished with Pye and also ghost-wrote several articles for Pye. Dyson's contribution was in answer to my exposé of Pye's Horsey claim. Dennis Pye had joined a pike fishing party to Ireland. This expedition included Fred Buller. Dyson wrote:

> *We were delighted to hear that Pye had got a twenty for the camera, but when we saw it! Anyway, we managed to weigh it when Dennis wasn't looking, and it weighed 14lb. odd. He let himself down, and not only spoiled a great record, his exaggeration obscured the record so completely that nobody – probably not even Dennis himself – knew what the true record was.*

This was virtually a mirror image of the incident on Horsey Mere.

The purpose of my description of my own experience in relation to one false claim is to illuminate the travails of becoming a pike ferret.

I neither sought, nor expected to be asked to take on the pike ferreting of dear old Omar. My book *Big Pike* was not intended to be an ego-trip of self-glorification, which puts it out of tune with some modern angling literature. I was pleased to pay a modest tribute to some fine pike anglers of the sixties, Edwin and Len Spencer to be sure, but also to that good friend, the Dutch angler, Franz Domhof, who committed suicide after a lifetime of intense pain following an immersion in arctic waters on the Russian convoys. My best friend in Norfolk was Harry Tallents, who wrote country-life stories under the pen-name of *Broadland Heron*.

There was another minor controversy in Omar's records. He believed that a small number of large pike were male fish. They appeared to shed milt when captured. Fred Buller assures me that no pike over 10 lb or so has been found with true milt. The mistake is because the large hen fish contained corrupted spawn which appeared to be milky.

Fred makes a compelling case. I confess that I accepted Fred's convincing statistics ... and yet ... nature does produce freaks. In the Middle Ages in rural France a cockerel laid an egg. It was duly charged in Court for witchcraft. On being declared guilty, on the orders of Holy Inquisition it was solemnly burned at the stake in Rouen market place where Joan of Arc met a similar fate.

We know some of our rivers suffer from what is called 'micro-pollution'. Waste from hospitals passes through the sewage system. Drugs used in chemo-treatment for cancer are believed to be changing the sex of fish in the rivers. When I began my work as a technician in the Department of Immunology I was given a word of good advice. A true scientist must never be dogmatic. He should have a firm belief in his own findings, but he should always have one smidgeon of doubt in his head ... 'it is possible that I may be wrong'. It is like the wisdom of Ancient Rome when a slave stood by the victor as he savoured his triumphal chariot ride through adoring crowds. The slave would whisper in his ear, 'Remember, you are only a man.'

Whilst remaining a firm supporter of the Pike Anglers Club I would like to sign a minority report on some of their rules. I was ever a heretic! The members believe that it is a conservation measure to return all captured fish to the water. It makes no conservation sense at all! Pike tend to over-breed small male jack-pike; nature needs a pruning hook. To allow members to have a controlled cull for the table is good for the overall health of the fishery as well as for contestants in cooking competitions. From Calais to Vladivostok pike are praised for their table quality, without harming their fisheries. I ate Quenelles de Brochet in the Loire valley without a qualm. It is one of the glories of the French cuisine. Yet the Loire still boasts adequate numbers of 'carnassiers'.

Like Martin Luther, 'here I take my stand. I can do no other.' Is there conservation value in preventing an angler from killing the catch of a lifetime to take to the dying art of taxidermy? It was with cynical eyes that I saw anglers rushing to fish a relatively short pool on a Kentish stream where a record barbel had been caught. Money is said to change hands to buy the location of specimen fish. My ferreting days proved to me that once the 'querencia'[2] of a big pike is known it shoots in and out of the water like a demented yo-yo until it goes belly-up. I would rather see it in a glass case.

My biggest bream was a horrid sight. It weighed eight-and-a-half pounds. It was coated in orange slime that stained my net, which also broke under its weight. The poor thing fought with all the panache of a wet lettuce. The fish itself was bible-black with mouth savagely distorted by scar tissue. It had been hooked many times.

Edwin Vincent persuaded me that live-baiting was wrong. I suspect that one day it will become illegal. Already I know

---

[2] This is a bull-fighting term. The bull takes up an area in the arena where it feels safe and secure.

that some angling clubs ban it. When I was a village lad in the Weald of Kent, when we discovered a roach pond we had to keep it secret. If the local farm workers knew about it they would quickly decimate its roach population for their live-baits. This happened on occasion. We village lads would discover a secret pond hollowed out by Huguenot refugees centuries ago. The word would leak out. On subsequent visits we would discover that gaunt farm workers were emptying the havens of the silver harvests we had discovered. The men clattered with their live-bait kettles from pond to pond. In the stark conditions of life of those days the pike were sought as a source of food. Isaak Walton would have been delighted.

Of course, live-baiting with Jardine's crude snap-tackle is cruel. Richard Walker graphically described how the live roach shuddered when the arm of a treble hook was pushed through its spine. Another objection is that thoughtless live-baiters return their injured bait-fish to the water where they become subject to fungal or bacterial infection, to spread amongst the other fish. The famous Taylor brothers, Joe and Fred, taught us long ago that pike can be caught on dead sea fish, sprats, mackerel and herring. My best pike-catch, thirteen in one session, was on mackerel baits. I should not be unhappy if one day a law were to be passed to make illegal live-baiting with multi-treble hooked rigs. We are fortunate that so far the anti-angling brigade has missed this controversy. These critics dare not admit that angling is a self-correcting sport, as witness the fact that we were banning lead-shot before legislation. We also banned knotted landing nets and keep nets which scoured the protective slime from fish. Gaffs were consigned to the torture chamber in the Tower of London.

My career as a specimen hunter ended when the *Fishing Gazette* died. Over the years I have watched carp fever save the fishing tackle trade. Fred Wilton took the mystique out of carp fishing. The carp was no longer the mastermind of the piscine world. Carp became so besotted with flavoured high-protein bait that they were as easy to catch as mentally retarded bream. Heavy pre-baiting raised them to incredible weights and grotesque shapes. You would get more fight if you foul-hooked a sack of spuds. The intensive stocking of still-water trout fisheries not only brought rainbow trout into double figures, but pike in reservoirs like Grafham and Chew came to believe that every day was Christmas Day with appropriate tame-fish dinners with all the trimmings. My own quest for a natural 3 lb roach was turned into disillusionment by the intense protein ground-baiting of lakes.

Anglers deserted natural rivers and crowded onto stocked lakes. Coarse fishermen adopted the artificial standards of the trout fisherman's 'put and take' philosophy where time is money. There came the legend of the bivvy behind the bivvy, each camper being rationed in time and space. When once I had to rise before the first peep of dawn to find a free swim on the Medway or Thames, now I could walk long stretches of bank without finding a fellow angler. The great organisations of the past, like the Thames Anglers Association, lost their membership and fisheries.

Does it matter? Probably not in practical terms. Our sport has always adjusted to changes in society. It survives. In a sense I won a selfish benefit. Before I moved to the North, every Saturday I fished the Medway. I had a wide choice of swims. Anglers who packed onto the banks of nearby stocked still-waters did not realise that the river was fishing better than I had ever known. For my wild brown trout fishing there were remote lakes and rivers which the rainbow-trout bashers ignored. No, I cannot complain.

Sometimes a tale of infinite sadness has to be told. Dear old Halford, when he lost his beloved Test fishery[3] he had to

---

[3] F. M. Halford, *An Angler's Autobiography*.

*In the early years, the Bucknall family at Keston Park.*

close the wicket-gate behind him for the last time. My companions have long since joined the great majority. The last time I went to Hickling the Broad was covered in Canadian pond weed and no one fished. The Heigham Sounds and West Hole were out of bounds. The Pleasure Boat Inn had new owners. That very same day Gwen Amies, the landlady, was going into a nursing home. I saw the back of the car as it took her away. I could not say 'goodbye'. Many years before, her husband, Alf, invited us to choose any drink we liked from the bar. He was saying 'goodbye', for he was on temporary leave from the cancer ward to which he had to return. He passed away a few days later. Edwin, too, has gone, as has George, the genial warden. I had no news of Jack Nudd who took me in his boat to beat the reed beds, to scare the sheltering pike into the open water.

That was the time the big storm came, as in Jean Ingelow's poem, 'The Lord that sent it, He knows all'. Prince Philip and his son Charles were flooded out from Whiteslea Lodge and their coot shooting was abandoned. Pike fishermen, coming down to breakfast, were astonished to see the Royal pair tucking in to sausage and bacon in the Pleasure Boat Inn. I bet they never enjoyed a better meal.

I shut my eyes and visualised Catfield Dyke as it was, shining like a steel ribbon in the evening sun whilst the pike harried the roachlings on the surface, their spoon-shaped speckled dorsal fins cleaving through the surface. The great days have gone, but this is the sport that allows you to conjure up golden memories by the winter fire, glass in hand. The ghosts will come to surround you, the pike men of long ago. If you take a deep breath there will come to you that musty smell, compounded of black ooze and stagnant water . . . lovely! I was there when I was young, learning my craft, and every year meeting the same two older men: the restaurateur from St Albans, Mr Thrale, and his dentist companion whose chewed natural rudd, Pflueger plug-bait had long since lost its paint. Yet he fished with nothing else and the pike still came to the bare wood.

It is a haunting, wintry landscape which the holiday folk never see. The wind moans through the sere reeds. You wake at first light, a pale light. The wind rattles the loose panes of the old pub. Below on the staithe, a party of ducks squabble over wet bread. You don't want to leave the snug bed, but you know you must. Before the sausages and bacon are frying you must catch your roach for bait and the cats will try to snatch them from your line as you swing them in. You know you will go, and Edwin grunts with approval as you swing out your bait properly on the centre-pin. You are master of the craft, now, and the pike will come. If, by chance, you see another angler spinning with a modern fixed-spool reel, you allow yourself a gentle sneer. You never use that coffee-mill yourself.

# 5

*The blackbird sings to him, 'Brother, brother,*
*If this be the last song you shall sing,*
*Sing well, for you may not sing another;*
*Brother, sing.'*

Julian Grenfell (1888–1915), 'Into Battle'

YOU MAY FIND the verse above to be a strange choice. It was written by a poet who became known as 'the Happy Warrior' when he died from shrapnel wounds in 1915.

My purpose is to show you another image, of poets who hated war so much that they had to go through enemy trenches with bayonet and grenade. Such men were Sassoon and Blunden, both decorated with the Military Cross.

Perhaps the modern image of a poet is of an unwashed, pimply youth with tangled hair, soiled and torn jeans and sandals. Poetry has become one of the many victims of the dumbing-down process which has numbed the brains of today's 'couch potatoes'. There is, though, a secret underground resistance movement, for when I heard that a local pub was inviting would-be poets to an evening of 'pints and verse' I found the room packed with 'all sorts and conditions of men', from stockbrokers to milkmen as well as some shy, elderly widows.

I suggested to the Minister of Culture that he might persuade the breweries to organise 'Poems and Pints' evenings throughout the land. 'Great idea,' he said and did nothing. I love poetry; my life would be drab without a fish-stained copy of *The Oxford Book of Modern Verse* which slips into a pocket of my fishing bag. When the fish have decided not to bite, I lie down in the shade, having taken my bottle of cider or Graves from Nature's fridge in the water, and I read until my eyelids grow too heavy to keep open.

In my green-shoot years I had an ambition to write poetry. For a few months the Muse favoured me with her presence. Then one day She flew out of the window, never to return. I have had to content myself with writing prose ever since. Times have changed since a crowd of eager readers tried to snatch the pages of Byron's *Childe Harold* while they were hot from the press. Poetry lovers creep about shame-faced today, hiding their slim volumes inside copies of the tabloid press.

I don't know if my head is worth being hunted but I felt flattered when a very old friend, Kenneth Robson, asked me to contribute a regular column to the *Fly Fishers' Journal*, which he edited. These contributions were to be entitled 'Jottings from my Log Book', which was another compliment as the renowned Mr Skues wrote a similar column years ago. Ken and I shared a secret love of poetry, now revealed. He was always generous with space. I sent him up to two thousand words in a time when other editors preferred to shrink writing space to make room for pretty pictures. That is another example of 'dumbing-down' and Ken scorned it even though he did carry enough photos and cartoons to balance the printed pages.

At first I was reluctant. I was not a member of the Fly Fishers' Club. It would have blown a hole through the family budget. I was doubtful about their 'men only' policy, but tolerance is a stronger influence in my life. I cannot recall how many articles I wrote for Ken over several years. But there came a sad time when he fell ill. His eyesight was also failing. I knew I had to write my last 'Jottings' for him. I guessed that a new editor would prefer 'modern ways' which did not suit our old-fashioned style. I decided to link our love of poetry with our love of fly fishing. I had to write to him in 24-point type to slide past his dry macular-diseased retinas. He rang to tell me how much he and his wife loved the article. It was the last time we spoke together. This is what I had written, and of all the prose I have contributed to angling magazines, this one gives me the greatest pride. It was to be my swansong for his Journal, too, for like Keats, 'mortality weighed heavily on me like unwilling sleep'. I felt honoured to have been included amongst the finest angling writers of our time. Please accept this as a modest memorial to a fine man, a firm friend and a skilled angler, Kenneth Robson.

*JOTTINGS FROM MY LOG BOOK, SUMMER 2007*

> *The men that live in North England,*
> *I saw them for a day.*
> *Their hearts are set upon vast fells.*
> *Their skies are fast and grey.*
> *And from their castle walls a man may see*
> *The mountains far away.*

One of my favourite poets, Hilaire Belloc, was so besotted with the South Country that he mildly disparaged those from the West, the Midlands and the North. When he grew old he vowed to build a house with a deep thatch on the high land by the sea shore, where songs of Sussex would be sung and the story of Sussex told. There would his poor soul be healed. There would he drink with those who were boys when he was a boy. I know how he felt, for the golden days of my boyhood were the two years I lived in a tiny hamlet on the Romney Marsh before the shadows of war fell across that magical and lonely landscape when Authority decreed that the most famous sheep in the world should be taken away from the invading barbarians ... and my mother and I had to leave with the other 'non-essential' folk. Now, sixty-five years later I still conjure up the memory of three of us, young boy anglers, bobbing for eels on a dyke near

Dymchurch, opposite the old slaughterhouse ... the memory brings a lump in my throat and unshed tears sting behind my eyelids.

I remember visiting a house in Sussex where lived the Bloomsbury Group, and looking from the window down to the Ouse, I mentioned to the guide that the sea-trout used to hang on the bend of the river as the tide was falling there, and I would fish the Queen of the Water fly to them. He said quietly, 'That is just where Virginia Woolf drowned herself.' She went down from the house, slipped some heavy stones into the pocket of her coat and slid into the water. I looked at the bitter winter-flow and felt myself shiver. Later, I strolled down to the familiar fishing place, and there was the old eel-bobber fishing in the old marsh way, with a great ball of wool tied to his line, and the worms wriggling to get free. The teeth of the eels would catch in the wool as they sought to snatch the worms, and they would never let go.

Now, should you think that poets are effeminate wastrels, think only of Sassoon and Blunden, both holders of the Military Cross on the Somme battlefield. True, they told Britain of the madness of war, but cowards they never were. And as for Belloc, his poem 'Tarantella' somehow reawakens in many of us the memoirs of a sad time when we were parted from someone we cared for in a mystical time and place which is frozen into a sad, sad memory. For all who suffered thus, we know how he felt in returning to the empty, forlorn Inn in the High Pyrenees from whence all had gone, too, leaving only the doom-laden sound of the far Aragonese waterfall booming through the empty halls. Was Miranda his lost love, I wonder? I do not know. When I read it, it reminds me of the irretrievable moment in time when we reach out to grasp the illusion of happiness, as perhaps it was meant to be before, metaphorically speaking, Adam stole the forbidden apple.

The words in a Bloch cantata have the ring of truth.

*Dreams without grief are always brief, and once broken, they come not again.*

The classical poets do not conform to that image of the knotted cravat, velveteen coat, the long curly locks, and the effeminate disposition. I have a portrait of Rupert Brooke which projected that image but he died a soldier's death at Gallipoli. Visualise Wilfred Owen, Siegfried Sassoon and Edmund Blunden storming enemy trenches with bayonet and grenade. The last two were both anglers from my native Weald. Yet Rupert Brooke was unfriendly to anglers, whilst Sassoon cast a fly on the River Teise at Lamberhurst where the Conningsby and Brandon families feuded in those rollicking pirate adventures of Jeffrey Farnol.

Blunden, strolling out from his father's schoolhouse in Yalding, would stare in amazement as a huge pike swirled in the weir pool when the miller opened the hatches. So poets are enmeshed with fishing, for even Yevtushenko sat down by the side of the carp angler when he returned to Zima Junction, that remote village in Siberia where he grew up.

Yet everyone's patriotic poet, Rupert Brooke, sympathised with the fish, not with the fisherman. His poem, simply called 'The Fish', is a marvel. He conveys us to the underwater world *where hope is fleet and thought flies after*. And in another poem he dreams up a Paradise for those fish which, suffering from the cruel persecution of anglers, transmigrate to a squamous Paradise after death . . .

*Oh! Never fly conceals a hook*
*Fish say, in that Eternal Brook . . .*
*. . . Unfading moths, immortal flies*
*And the worm which never dies.*
*And in that Heaven of all their wish.*
*There shall be no more land, say fish.*

The legend remains. Rupert Brooke: almost the Establishment Poet, for the legend was made by his early death in that Great War, and his memory, enshrined in those words *'If I should die'*, conjures up the horror of Flanders fields, poppies and *lions led by donkeys*. Yet I regret his early death, for here and there in his poetry I discover a more discerning, even cruel pen which might not have been popular in the drawing rooms of the middle class. Such is his imagining of the domestic bliss in the Menelaus and Helen household as the years went by after the fall of Troy.

> *Menelaus bold*
> *Waxed garrulous, and sacked a hundred Troys*
> *'Twixt noon and supper. And her golden voice*
> *Got shrill as he grew deafer. And both were old.*

So, Brooke surviving the Great War might well have excoriated our sport in a ruthless way, such was his magic with words. And I doubt he would have thanked God to be matched to that hour.

Two poets survived. I described before how our stream, the Teise, has a dead poet at each end: Sassoon, teasing trout on the Teise where it meandered through the golf course at Lamberhurst, and Blunden at Yalding. You will find Blunden's verse engraved on a glass pane in the splendid church there. And Sassoon hunted the fox across the Weald and wrote his ironic memoirs of a fox-hunting man, for he had trouble in the tying of his stock.

This is a nostalgic exercise for me. It would displease Belloc, for I have deserted my native Weald to live in Upper Teesdale. I am jotting down my thoughts on angling and poetry for I need them both. Bernard Venables told me how much he worshipped words. No matter how well he wrote prose, nothing rouses the small hairs on the back of my neck so much as a well-crafted poem. This is why the fish-stained slim volume slides out of my fishing bag when the trout are dour. I am poised on a rock above the Northern river, reading Belloc's opinion that I should not be in such a bleak landscape when I should rather be amongst his well-wooded walks on the Downs.

Yet I have a twinge of sympathy with him. There's a memory-flash of the Elmley marshes on the Kent coast where I buried myself in the reed-beds to marvel at the great marsh harrier, jinking from one wing to the other. Another memory conjures up the image of the Teise stream at dusk. I am putting a dry Coachman to a rising trout. I know the exact spot. I am perched precariously halfway up the bank just above Small Bridge. It is a left-handed throw to the fish making dimples beneath a low branch of the overhanging willow tree. I have to be perfectly relaxed or I shall fluff the cast. I can just see the tops of the two church towers on opposite sides of the stream at Goudhurst and Horsmonden. The village bell-ringers used to talk to each other across the valley with brazen tongues ... just as I was about to be overwhelmed by sadness a merlin darted after a small bird across the meadow of my new abode in the North Pennines.

Yes, Mr Belloc, the North Countree has its compensations. The Grey Men have not yet pushed their concrete mixers up this valley.

And yes, Mr Belloc. I understand the language of '*the far waterfall like doom*'. I hear the sound of the silent footfalls in the desolate halls of that deserted Inn, where Aragon is '*a torrent at the door*'. For those who love poetry will feel it when it plucks at the heartstrings, when it reminds us of a lost time, when once we felt ourselves to be so near to what might have been ... if only, like Omar of old, we had dared to rebuild Life nearer to the heart's desire ... that is when we need the consolation of the trout stream where sorrows can be banished from the mind. That was the escape which

Patrick Chalmers longed for through the dire days of winter when he was yearning for spring to break so that he could rush to the river to meet the first March Brown. It is not only to escape from present woes; it is also to bury past regrets. That is why we go fishing.

# 6

*And when the war is done and youth stone dead*
*I'd toddle safely home and die – in bed.*
                              Siegfried Sassoon

LET ME INTRODUCE YOU to Flight-Sergeant McDowell.
He was a fighter pilot in 11 Group, which bore the brunt
of the Battle of Britain in the South-East. My father had
joined the RAF Volunteer Reserve in 1938. He became an
expert in cannibalising Spitfires from the wreckages of those
which fell victim to 'Emils', as the German fighter planes
were known. McDowell was one of 'the Few' in his
squadron who succumbed, after he had shot down eleven
enemy planes. As the crash cost him a leg he was invalided
out of the Service. At that time my mother and I were still
living in the Weald, so my father rented out to the disabled
hero our small terrace house in West Wickham, a house
known as 'One Tree' as a formidable oak stood in the front
garden. Like Charles Stuart after the Battle of Worcester, I
was to owe my life to an oak tree.

Neighbours from Hell are not a new TV invention. There
was one next door to that suburban house. He protested to
Authority continually at the noise of the ex-pilot's artificial
limb on the stairs, so much so that our tenant was forced to
move. By then my father had been posted to South Africa.
My mother seized the opportunity to move back to her
family home.

Now, in my seventies, I am one of those 'old farts', as
described by my daily newspaper, which accuses us of
boring the pants off younger folk in the bar-rooms with tales

of a planet which long since swam beyond their ken. If those younger folk could only leave the pub through a time-warped door, although they would be in the same street they know, they would not recognise it. Each house would have a pile of rubble at its front door, and a pig-bin in which kitchen refuse was collecting swarms of bluebottles. The windows had no glass; they were covered in thick canvas. Blast from flying bombs had stripped plaster from the walls, glass from the windows, and residents would live behind these first-aid repairs erected by gangs of Irish labourers. Instead a glazed look comes into their eyes when any senior citizen tries to convey to them how in that time he walked abroad with eye and ear anxiously cocked towards the killing sky.

It was a strange time for schoolboys. The younger teachers had been called to the war and older, retired ones coaxed back into harness. They inflicted on us the teaching methods of the Victorian age, learning by rote and parsing sentences into incomprehensible grammatical terms. Even that did not last. As the intensity of the bombing increased the schools were evacuated to distant shires. It struck home to the private school to which my mother sent me, one of those bucket shops which sprang up in war-time to cash in on homeless kids or those whose parents had been riven apart. Those of us who stayed behind in 'Flying Bomb Alley' wandered footloose through the streets and nearby woods and fields.

One night I stood at our front door to watch a row of six of these flame-tailed missiles chunter over the roof of our house, each with a warhead of 1000 lb of explosive, enough to knock down a terrace of houses. The trick was to wait for the engine to stall. You had thirty seconds to throw yourself flat or crawl under anything looking like shelter.

Our turn came at two o'clock in the morning. Foolishly I had refused to join my mother to sleep in an iron cage in the drawing room, a crude table of iron surrounded by grills known as a Morrison shelter. Foolhardy, I slept in my truckle bed in the small front bedroom with its glass cupola of a window. I was awakened by the customary sound of a spluttering tractor motor as the missile approached. When overhead the thing stuttered to a halt. I had time to drop onto the floor and roll under the bed. I almost made it, when the world crashed in through the front wall. Near to a bomb you hear no bang, just a rushing noise as the air is driven out and then tears in again. I felt choked by dust; blood was streaming down my nose. I fumbled around in the darkness, finding something cloth-like to bind my head. It seemed hours before torches were shining; someone was calling my name amid the strident clamour of an ambulance bell. Sometimes at two in the morning I wake with a bell ringing in my ears. I say to my wife, 'There's someone at the door.' There never is.

My cuts were inspected. It was declared that these were only 'flesh wounds' – but my flesh, I thought – and I was dispatched to the First Aid Post. There, a St John's man stitched my head. As the flying bombs still chugged overhead so did I view with alarm his wobbling needle as it went up past my eyes. God, where's he going with that? I thought. They took me to my grandparents' house nearby. Ours was uninhabitable, though the stout oak tree had prevented its complete destruction.

Next day I scoured the rubble which had been my bedroom. Half-buried in plaster was my shirt, stiffened and blackened with dried blood. It was this I had wound around my head. The mattress of my bed was shredded with shards of glass. I would have died there. In the corner, unharmed, was my fishing rod. Over fifty years later, when turning the pages of my beloved *Fishing Gazettes*, I came across a report from a young army officer who was serving in the Ashanti wars. Being sent out with his companions into the bush to locate a party of comrades who had not returned to camp, he discovered their remains. They had been surprised by a native war-party and they were butchered as they slept. Their modest bivouacs had been incinerated, yet there, rising like a phoenix from the ashes, he found the officer's Hardy rod, still in fine fettle. This was a testament to the quality of British workmanship, he wrote. The flesh and blood of his comrades failed the same test; not even their stiff upper-lips survived.

It was decreed that I should return to the Weald to help a friendly farmer at Horsmonden. At first, as a wounded hero with an arm in a sling, sympathetic white bandages around my head and arms, I was quite attractive to the village girls. As wounds healed and the bandages fell away, alas my pulling powers waned. When the very last dressing came off, they disappeared altogether, and worse, there being no schooling, I was expected to work on the farm for sixpence an hour.

I was presented to the farmer. He looked me up and down. He said: 'Farm boys! Ar, one boy is one boy. Two boys is 'arf a boy. And three boys is no boy at all!'

Fruit farming is fun. Some days I pulled a rope to make steel drums clatter off the birds from the cherry trees. Other times there was the back-breaking drag of pea-picking, joining a long line of village women, clad in their filthy aprons, who kept on calling, 'Hurry up, Geoff, catch up.'

One day we were in the orchard, on the slope of a hill. I was using a pitchfork to lift swards of long grass on to the trailer. Glancing up I was startled to see a parachutist drifting down into the valley below. 'A Jerry,' cried the farmer. 'I'll get the gun.' We ran down the hill, he with his twelve bore, myself with the pitchfork.

'Don't you stick that thing into him,' he shouted to me. 'If he gives us any trouble I'll shoot the bugger!'

The airman was crumpled with his 'chute. He shrugged it

off when we approached him, saying in broad Yankee accent. 'Oh hell, we all got shot up over Bremen. Couldn't land. Had to bail out.'

We took him back to the farmhouse, gave him a cure-all cup of tea whilst the farmer phoned the local policeman. The airman wanted to give the farmer the prized silk 'chute but the policeman stuffed it into his van, claiming it had to be saved as Government property.

'Ted's wife and daughters will be having green silk knickers for the next few years,' said the farmer.

I had been billeted in the village. The man of the house was an ex-soldier who had lost a leg on the Somme and was so bitter about the second war that two Special Branch men came down to interrogate the local people as to his suitability to be locked up under Regulation 18B. Everyone testified to his loyalty. He was left alone. His own father had been a master ploughman who habitually won the championships of ploughing with heavy horses. His brass awards hung in chains on either side of the fireplace. It was rumoured that before ploughing matches he could be seen skulking in the bushes to spy on the practice sessions of his competitors. He told me of a farm pond, virtually unfished during the war, where lived big roach and rudd. By now both the farmer and I had decided that I was not fit to be a son of the soil, so I was paid off. I passed the idle summer days in cycling around the villages in search of promising ponds.

With myself in rural exile, my father in South Africa assembling Spitfires for the Desert Campaign, the schools evacuated to distant parts, and my mother in hospital with pneumonia, my academic career ended. I suppose if we meet in the second life I will have to stand the jovial Reichsmarschall Goering a drink in the Golden Gates bar to thank him for my education in fruit growing and the care of apple trees. I will overlook the fact that he was trying to kill me.

Today I rejoice in a splendid Peasgood Nonsuch tree in my garden. If you are unfamiliar with this Old English bearer of huge apples, let me tell you that its fruit cooks to a froth and doesn't give anything away in flavour to the Bramley. A neighbour was so entranced by sight of my blushing scrumpies that she sent her young daughter round, clutching a banknote.

'Could you sell my mum a pound of your apples?' she implored me. I picked one of the Peasgoods for her, and said: 'Please give this to your mum with my compliments and tell her it's a gift as I won't cut one of my apples in half for anyone!'

The Weald was still a dangerous place. The guns which had circled London had brought down flying bombs onto the houses of the Home Guard gunners. The weapons were moved down into the Weald. When a flying bomb crossed the coast its predicted course was marked by the shooting of yellow flares into the sky to warn the gunners. The flying bombs ran their passage to London through a storm of shrapnel. This shower of red-hot steel shards hurtled down to earth, each splinter capable of ripping off the arm or smashing through the brain pan.

I had discovered a large furnace pond. It had been created near to the village in days long gone when they made cannons in the Weald. From the air such ponds look like pairs of trousers. The smelting works had crumbled away though the tiny furnace brook, the home of grey wagtails and fingerling trout, still chuckled its way out of the lake. Halfway along one bank was a long, rickety landing stage. Behind it was a meadow with a battery of anti-aircraft guns. I could see the gunners relaxing in chairs, tea mugs in hand, some reading comics.

One hot noonday, I had bought a pint of rough cider in the village. My mother had come to stay with us to recuperate. She had established a routine whereby I would collect her spiritual needs at the pub, so no questions were asked by the landlord. I collected my tackle and some bread. I walked down the lane to the pond, and, scrambling along the landing stage, I perched over the water. With a high summer thirst, I gulped down cloudy nectar and watched my float settle by the shoals of rudd. No air moved. Relentlessly the sun beat down on my uncovered skull. My head became swimmy. Suddenly, up went the yellow flare, the gunners shouted, their seats flew all ways; the comics were strewn on the grass as they ran up to the guns. The flying bomb came right over the lake through a crescendo of bursting shells. It escaped, showing its burning tail-flame in contempt. The shrapnel rained down around me, ripping strips of wood from the landing stage, tearing branches from the trees, and churning the gravy-coloured water into creamy foam. I had never been so scared in my life; I had nowhere, no time to run. Seconds after it was all over, the lake returned its calm smile to the sun, and I was standing with racing heart, thumping head and shaking knees.

I crawled back on all fours along that landing stage. There, on the grassy bank stood a large water tank on brick piles. I thought I could creep under it next time. I fished nearby. That evening a gunner came down to fish. He was a Staffordshire man with a superb match-fishing outfit. This was when I saw my first fixed-spool reel, the Allcock's Stanley. I marvelled at how easily he threw his toothpick float from the tiny bobbin-spool towards the distant lily pads. This is where the rudd were. Before long his float slid away and the silver and vermilion fish, gaily arrayed like Saracens, spluttered towards his net. I watched, enraptured.

I never forgot that wonder-reel. It had the promise of defeating that frustrating limitation, small boy with short rod. Years later I went into a London store to buy my first fixed-spool reel.

'You don't want that sort of rubbish,' the assistant told me. 'This will serve you for a lifetime, the best reel you can buy.'

It was a Rapidex centre-pin, though it might have been called a 'Flick 'em'. He did me a favour. This past Saturday I was on the Medway at Tonbridge, staring down at my old Rapidex and wondering why I ever thought to change. I love that reel. It's a lifetime reel.

The summer of 1944 waned into a sun-gilded autumn when the air was heavy with the smoke from roasting hops mixed with the dusty pollens of meadow grass. I had discovered another pond shrouded in trees, but distant from the guns. The westering sun was beginning to fade. The fish were lolling where a shadow lay across the water. My mother, recuperating from her illness, was reading on the grassy knoll behind when I hooked the biggest roach of my life. I had it on the surface, an eye-twinkling silver dinner-plate. Hermann Goering chose that very moment to send one of his infernal machines over our heads, and in a panic, staring heavenwards, I pulled too early, I pulled too hard. The richest treasure of my fishing life sank silently into the depths, leaving a flaccid line on the surface and myself, a groaning heap on the bank.

Those golden days were to end. Distant Grey Men with souls of lead, they were to move us to Hunton, to the Tudor manor house at Buston. The new weapon from the German arsenal was launched, the V2 rocket which plunged down from the stratosphere, unheralded, with awesome destruction in its nose. One evening, standing on a hill at Cox Heath, I saw a rocket launched, probably from the French coast. A ribbon of white smoke-trail was etched against a cobalt-blue sky. The curvature of the earth must have acted like a magnifying glass. It ascended upwards to the vault of heaven where it died in a brilliant flash, high above the earth. Seconds later the characteristic double-bang shook the air. It was the drum roll of my departure from the Weald and the vale of the horsemen who rode by long ago.

Those were the green days before high-protein baits and 'boilies' had been invented. We believed that carp were endowed with super-intelligence. They scrutinised each offering with suspicion. The slightest sign of line or hook, they sauntered away, treating the bait with disdain. Bernard Venables described the dedicated carp fisher as a man with a dreamy far-away look in his eyes who gazed into depths of timeless hours by the lake without so much as a tremor to his line. Their quarry was the mastermind of fish. Their hero was a man called Buckley who caught huge carp from a lake near Heanor, fish so wide in girth that he gaffed them and took them away on a handcart to be set-up. Most of us were unwilling to pass away endless hours in the futile quest for carp until Walker's forty-four pounder from Redmire proved that specimen carp were not geniuses; they were only human after all.

A new mystique arrived, complete with its own jargon. I was seduced. I sent off for my 'James Mark IV' carp rod. So busy was the Ealing manufacturer that the varnish had hardly dried on the superb miracle of dark split cane with maroon whippings when it arrived. I studied how to prepare the bait of balanced crust which was a sliver torn from a new loaf stuck onto a keel of soft paste, so designed that it rested gently even on the softest silt. I mastered the physics of the thermal stratification of lakes in summer whereby a layer of warm water floated on top of a cold one. The two layers would tilt with the prevailing wind forming a deep wedge of tepid comfort along the windward shore where the carp loved to lounge through the dark hours. A new generation of fishermen had arrived, the Specimen Hunters. I joined them.

We had our own biannual conferences thanks to the Department of Zoology at Liverpool University. The scientists gave us the benefits of their research into the ways of fish and fisheries.

The birds and the bees were for the birds. We ignored the delights of Nature; ignored were the tiny pipistrelles flickering through the twilight, the tawny owls on hunting flight. No, we were glued to our electronic bite alarms, hypnotised by that red eye of the monitor, glowing like a miniscule Cyclops.

One day I answered an advertisement in the angling press and found myself with other syndicate members being escorted along the bank of a carp lake in Sussex. This was Wadhurst Park. The fish were not the grotesque gut-buckets we know today. They were slim, wild fish which scalded line from the reel when hooked.

We had our specially designed hooks, large and wide-gaped. They fulfilled Marryat's ageless dictum for the perfect hook, 'the temper of a saint, the penetration of a prophet and the strength to stop a runaway bull in a ten acre field'.

This was the time when I had been recently married, and saddled myself with a mortgage. I could scrape together enough funds to join the syndicate. I had succumbed to temptation. I had bought the latest miracle of technology, a Felton Crosswind fixed-spool reel. I could not afford the electric bite alarm. It was decreed that night fishing was a necessity. My method was simple. I chose a swim between bushes, cast out my bait at dusk and settled down into a garden chair, the rod across one arm, the line resting on my forefinger. It was fatiguing, with the blessing that the slightest twitch at the bait registered immediately. I changed the bait every quarter of an hour, timed by the clock on a chapel above the lake.

I had experienced the panache of a hooked wild carp when bream fishing on the Hythe Military Canal just below the ruins of Stutfall Castle. I was fishing with the Stanley, my first fixed-spool reel. You know that the early fixed-spool reels would only cast ultra-fine lines of woven thread, mine being of about 2 lb breaking strain. I was consoled by the salesman's soothing words, 'A bigger fish can't break you, thanks to the slipping clutch. Set it lighter than the resistance of your line.' I popped the old Rapidex back in the cupboard; I was a modern angler at last.

No problem at all with the silver bream which were intoxicated by my bread paste. Then arrived the carp. The line sizzled off the slipping clutch; oh yes, it did work. The salesman forgot to tell me that it would not stop slipping! The carp steamed into a bed of lilies some twenty yards away.

That night at Wadhurst Park I hooked two carp. The first one taught me a lesson. I had set the clutch too lightly. I felt the line twitching on my finger, then sliding away. I struck. The reel sang its song. The fish streaked straight into a tangle of tree roots. I sent the usual Anglo-Saxon imprecations to the Gods above, tightened the clutch, re-baited and tried again. Hours passed with no further activity until the sun began to peep over the low dam wall at the far end of the lake. Again the digital nerve endings were set a-tingling. And this time I made no mistake, turning the fish just short of the sunken branches. Soon I was gazing down on my first carp, a muscled wild warrior, the early morning light gleaming on its chain-mail flanks.

The magic has gone from carp fishing. The carp has been demoted from being a super brain. It is pumped up to grotesque weight by high-protein bait. At first I joined the ranks of lager-saturated bivvy-boys, only to be stirred from drink-sodden slumber by the clamour of an electronic bite alarm, signalling that Old Fred had been self-hooked for the umpteenth time. Horsed in like a sack of spuds, the poor old thing has the hook removed from its scarred lips before being tossed into a sack for its night-time prison sentence.

Eventually poor Old Fred will tire of life, who can blame him, and his bloated corpse will stink in the shallows.

What do I miss? The lake no longer holds a mystery. Each named fish comes in and out of the water like a yo-yo. Every big carp is known and named from the day it is smuggled in a wet sack from France and offered as an entry fee by its owner in seeking to join the syndicate. Yes, fishing reflects the values of Society, God help us all!

Keith Linsell

# 7

*Where are your foes, where are they?*
*You'd have trouble finding them again ...*
*Ah, there they go so blandly*
*cordial with their nodding heads.*
Yevgeny Yevtushenko, 'Other Times'

THE TIME MACHINE is on wing again. It deposits you in front of the gates of a military airfield. It is 1948. You are lucky to catch a glimpse of me, a humble corporal, passing the Guard House on the way out of camp, giving a friendly wave to a Flight Sergeant of the RAF police who sits in the open window. I am carrying a fishing rod and a bag of tackle. The policeman glances quickly to left and right. Seeing that there is no one else in sight, he gives me a nod, a wink and a slight wave of his hand to indicate that I can pass.

I am mildly astonished when I read the comments of politicians that it would be a salutary lesson to wild young-sters to give them a taste of the discipline of National Service. My experience is that this would be counter-produc-tive. And having been amused often by revelations of sleaze in the corridors of power, I would observe with Juvenal: *Nemo repente fuit turpissimus* (no one ever reached the climax of vice at one step).

Having been in the Army Cadets in the war and adopted as a mascot by Dad's Army when the schools were closed by intensive bombing, I soon realised that military life was a thieves' kitchen. My first experience was the Sunday morning forays with the Signal Section of the local Home Guard. We only had the technology of the Great War. We laid miles of field telephone cables around the local commons.

The days following, local households were sporting new clothes lines and aerials for radios. Painstakingly we tested the remaining lines to find the gaps, and then repaired them.

On being drafted into the Air Force in 1947 it took me about twelve months to learn from the 'Old Sweats' who had signed on before the war that survival depended on how to make the system work for oneself instead of the other way round – the latter was the province of the 'keen types'. It took another six months to convert the RAF into my personal service; the competition was fierce. Everyone was at it. We knelt at the feet of the regular senior NCOs to learn how to master the art of column-dodging. It would take another book to describe our application of the lessons, a minor version of that hilarious film, *Private's Progress*. I should have to 'take the Fifth'.

At least I did not indulge in outright criminality as practised by my predecessors, for on discovering a hole in the boundary fence, cleverly concealed behind our Sick Quarters, I was told in confidence that previously the recovery annexe had been used as a bordello where sex-starved airmen were comforted by village maidens who were smuggled in by two long-departed corporals – at a price, of course. It all fell apart when one of these ladies was pregnant and her indignant father was berating a nonplussed green medical officer straight from medical school. I suspect that after a few years of a reintroduced National Service we would experience the delights of a far more sophisticated crime wave than mere antisocial behaviour. What else could they do? It was impossible to find sufficient occupation for a service which, in peacetime, far exceeded the needs of the country. Only at harvest time were we useful in helping the farmers make stooks of their corn sheaves.

I was unlucky enough to be stationed at a training camp in Lincolnshire. From the balcony of the Sick Quarters I used to blow enormous soap bubbles. They floated as multi-hued miracles over the heads of the farm workers in the neighbouring fields. They gazed upwards in amazement at the glittering array, streaming for miles across the wold. I had to let them know how their taxes were being spent.

Those Authoritarians who ran things there were neurotic survivors from the prison camps of Singapore. They felt keenly the imaginary contempt of those who wondered at the largest surrender to inferior forces made by British armed services. In peacetime they thought the drill books to be their Bible. They were frustrated by the medical branch where I worked. They condemned it as an untouchable empire within an empire. It revelled in its own strategy of evading practically everything to do with discipline.

The secret was to collect a sheaf of chits signed by a gullible Medical Officer. You would have the unshorn locks of a poet. Your chit explained that owing to dandruff you were forbidden to undergo the military crew-cut. Your thick crêpe-soled shoes, known as 'brothel creepers', were covered by a chit sympathetically describing your fallen arches, and excusing you from marches and morning parades. A touch of conjunctivitis was reason enough for your sunglasses. When stopped by a 'snowdrop' (RAF policeman, not renowned for a high IQ), you hauled the sheaf of chits from your pocket and riffled through them to select the appropriate one. Appropriate to the alleged misdemeanour.

My problem was where to conceal my fishing gear. Being the corporal in charge of a barrack room of recruits, the truckle bed in my small room at the end of the dormitory was permanently laid out for kit inspection, as I never slept there. I had a comfortable bed in the WAAF's ward (we had no WAAFs there). I was next to the officers' ward where our Flight Sergeant slept (sick officers were treated in their married quarters). You see, hospital blankets and sheets are more comfortable than standard issue of 'biscuits' and coarse linen. In the barrack room my locker had to be left open for inspection. It was not meant to be used as an angler's den. In the end I tucked my rod, reel and gear away in a dark corner of the Sick Quarters. The huge advantage of a system where nearly everybody is playing by his own rules is that no one dare be a 'grass'. Mutual deterrent. That's how it works.

The undiscovered hole in the fence was used by me in the evening, to slip out to a local canal for a spot of bream fishing. On returning at dusk I was horrified to find that Authority had repaired the gap in the perimeter fence. This was the unofficial entrance to the previous corporals' 'knocking shop', but the unfortunate bun discovered in a villager's daughter's oven was, metaphorically speaking, used to block up the hole. I would have to chance my arm through the main gate, running the gauntlet past the guard-room. I did have one ace in the hole though, a 'snowdrop' corporal who obviously had a peptic ulcer which he was forced to conceal for fear of being diagnosed and sent packing back to Civvy Street. We kept him secretly supplied with antacid tablets in return for little favours like overlooking '252' charge sheets sent in by his zealous comrades on the railway stations. As luck would have it, as I tried to slink unnoticed past the guardroom, the grim figure of the police Flight Sergeant appeared and signalled me to approach him. I could not conceal the rod from him.

He pushed his face close to mine. He opened wide his mouth and my nostrils were assailed by the warm breath of the south, the stench of garlic and cheap red wine. He expelled so much air that I expected to gaze right down his throat to see the chunks of illicit steak floating around on a lake of booze.

'You're late,' he bellowed. 'Where's your pass?'

'I don't have a pass, Chiefy,' I confessed tremulously.

'Don't call me Chiefy, I'm not an effing Red Indian,' he screamed. 'What's that you are carrying?'

'I've been fishing,' I quavered. He stepped back.

'Come inside, Corporal!' he rapped out.

I crept into the guardroom. I'm for it now, I thought, visions of days of jankers.[1] He took me into his office, and closing the door, he turned to me with the ghost of a smile which almost returned him to the ranks of fallible humanity. The third degree began. He asked: 'Now tell me, exactly where have you been fishing?'

'On the canal at Hibaldstow,' I confessed.

'I haven't been able to find a decent place anywhere round here. What did you catch? What bait did you use, bread or worms? Come on. Cough it up.'

I revealed my secret swim by a canal a mile or two distant, where I had been catching so many choice bream that time passed by unremarked, making me late back to camp.

'Wait here. I've something to show you,' he said. He disappeared in the direction of the cells. Minutes later he returned bearing rod, reel and fishing bag. 'Would you look through this stuff to see if it's suitable for that canal?' I checked it through, recommended some lighter line and smaller hooks to nylon and directed him to Nobbs' tackle shop at Lincoln. I told him about the raft which came up the River Witham into the city of a weekend to collect anglers who were dropped off at chosen swims along the bank.

'Right, you can go now ... but sponge that fish slime off your trousers!'

I reflected that rules about the storage of tackle were more relaxed in the guardroom. Later, I found him occupying 'my swim' by the canal's lock-gate. 'Privilege of rank!' he smirked. But I didn't need the hole in the fence again.

---

[1] A form of tedious punishment, of reporting morning and evening to the guardroom in full marching order.

My inglorious military service was followed by a brief interlude in the murky world of politics. On demobilisation I
faced the dilemma of choice of career, but a bespoke one
was to hand. My family formed a coterie of what elsewhere
would have been considered as 'old shirts' in the Labour
movement. My grandfather, in his youth, had pounded the
pavements of Battersea, canvassing for Saklatvala, one of the
ILP[2] pioneers. My parents elected to work for the orthodox
Labour Party. Due to years of faithful service, they thought
there was enough 'piston' owing to start me up the greasy
pole of a political career. Unluckily, I had inherited my
grandfather's questioning mind so before long I was in
trouble. In politics 'pats on the back' on your way upwards
can become soft spots for the knives on your return journey
downhill.

All went well at first. I took on the grass-root job of local
Party secretary, and thence upwards through the regional
councils until I was summoned to the Foreign Office. There
was some patronage on offer for promising youngsters. The
Foreign Secretary, Herbert Morrison, asked me to join a
student delegation to a European conference at the new
Assembly of Europe's building at Strasbourg. He also
appointed me to a standing committee of UNESCO in
London where I sat next to a charming old General in the
Salvation Army.

This has little to do with fishing except insofar as my
tendency towards escapism threw me a lifeline when I discovered that I lacked the emotional stamina to survive a way of
life so accurately described by the French as '*un panier aux
crabes*'. How briefly to account for an interlude where I
escaped three resolutions to expel me from the Party?

---

[2] The Independent Labour Party for those gullible folk who fondly believed
that socialists had a right to Freedom of Thought.

The early fifties, that was when the 'Hard Left', having lost its two Communist MPs (Willie Gallagher in Clydeside and Phil Piratin in Stepney), realised that the only way to influence Government policy was to infiltrate the Labour Party, taking on those sordid jobs which no one else would relish. The next step was to surround themselves with a weird collection of malcontents, woolly-minded pacifists, and gullible pro-Soviet enthusiasts and so on. This would then give them control over local Parties and District Trades Councils, eventually going on to win over the National Conference. They achieved this, with opposing bloc-vote, card-carrying Trade Union barons hurling abuse at each other, like dinosaurs bellowing across a primeval swamp. Hence Gaitskell's famous but futile 'fight, fight and fight again' speech.

Strange people drifted into suburban 'bedsits'. God knows where they came from. Soon they had taken over ward organisations and local Parties. Obstacles like me had to be cleared from their route. I occupied positions they wanted. So the kangaroo courts were formed.

Unfortunately they never quite gained a majority, so I survived until my stamina's shelf-life gave out. I tore up my Party card. My meteoric political career lasted barely two years. At last the battles reached the national stage and media, with the Militant movement bursting out of Liverpool. They made the Labour Party unelectable for two decades. Like the fire-encircled scorpion, they stung themselves to death. They did me a favour. They proved that a political career was not for me. And in an oblique way they helped me along the alternative pathway where fishing became a way of life.

I did not realise this at the time. It started at that Strasbourg conference. Although I had a casual interest in French, I shared my billet in the University with a sympathetic member of the German Social Democratic Party who had lost a leg in the war. I made friends with a Ukrainian nationalist who had evaded Stalin's Gulags, only to fall victim years later to the cyanide pistol of a KGB assassin. I left Strasbourg with a determination to become fluent in French, Spanish and German, and I was converted to the European ideal.

They say that as one door closes another one opens. I had been reading the French angling magazine, *La Pêche et Les Poissons*. Speculatively, I submitted an article entitled '*Lettre d'Angleterre*' in which I described the differences of fishing methods between our two countries. The editor, Jérôme Nadaud, a sophisticated bearer of two Purdies when visiting Britain, invited me to write a regular column in his magazine.

The BBC picked up on this. Would I undertake a radio programme to invite French anglers to come to Britain? Would I not! The interviewer arrived at my house, complete with tape recorder. After the work was done he explained how he came to England in the war. He was a sea fisherman, a commercial one. The Germans allowed him to put to sea with his crew under an armed guard. One day they set forth, ostensibly to fish. Beyond land, they popped the guard into the sea and set course for freedom.

My activities had attracted the attention of some French manufacturers of fishing equipment. They were seeking export markets. Their problem was that many products did not suit our market. I had been working as a technician for the Wellcome Research Foundation and, although recently married, I decided that it was time to leave that firm, to set up my own business as an agent for the French manufacturers. Firstly, though, I had to go to the factories in France to design hooks, rods, floats and other impedimenta to suit our own fishing ways. Fishing really had become my way of life, albeit a risky one at first. My message to any would-be escapists who read this book is this: be sure you escape into a way of life you enjoy. I did.

I fear that I drifted into angling politics by accident.

Colonel James H. Ferguson became Director of the Salmon & Trout Association in 1984. It is fair to describe this association as the governing body of game fishing.

On paper it has local branches in most counties of the UK. In spite of earlier sterling work by Charles Jardine the Kent branch had fallen on hard times. The Director came into my city shop one day. He asked me if I could help resuscitate the county branch. I had to tell him that my business put too many demands on my time. If retirement came to me whilst I was still active, then I would do my best.

The popularity of the fishing tackle trade boomed in the late seventies. After this golden time it seemed as if Blake's 'invisible worm which flies in the night' had begun to gnaw at the kernel of our sport. I was so bemused at failing interest that I collected the statistics of rod licence sales. It was a gloomy picture. Those sales were declining by roughly 10% each year. The reasons were inexplicable, though it seemed to be a combination of several factors. It was the day of the couch potato who preferred watching to doing. The silver screen shone in the darkened room.

Granddads had always been stalwarts of our sport. When fathers were working such long hours that they could not take their sons down to the river, grandpa stepped in. Now the elderly folk discovered that the value of their pensions was being eroded by Government policy. Angling lost two generations, one of which was the seed-corn for the future.

My two fishing tackle shops were hit by one-way traffic systems where parking wardens swooped on our customers even before they had time to pick up their bait boxes. In 1992 it was time for me to put up the shutters and like Michael Henchard of old, I paid off my debts and wambled off into the sunset. I was then reminded of my promise to resurrect the former Kent branch of the S&TA. I was lucky to have the support of a friend, Colin North, who had been a superb competition fly fisherman, twice being chosen to fish in the England team.

We advertised an inaugural meeting at Bewl Reservoir. I wound up as Secretary and Organiser whilst Colin took on the job of Chairman. We had one of the most supportive committees I have ever witnessed. Without the shelter of their shield wall our standard would have been trampled down in the battles which followed. Within a few months we had raised the membership of the branch from sixty to over three hundred. We had not realised what sort of an organisation we had joined.

We were confronted with the truth at the first recruiting booth we opened at the majestic Agricultural Show at Detling.

The post-war generations of still-water trout anglers threw at us the image of the Association's elitist past. The Association had earned the reputation of having little interest in humble trout fishermen. Its influence at Westminster was directed at preserving the interests of land-owning salmon fishermen. The Association's administration list read like the pages of *Who's Who*. None of the ruling council and officers had been democratically elected. The Kentish Fishermen and the Fishermen of Kent declared war. We were going to campaign to win for subscription-paying members the right to nominate and vote. We did not realise how stark and bitter would be the battle to drag the mildewed Victorian beldame of patrimony into the modern world.

At least the new Director, Chris Poupard promised us a working party. He warned us that our modernisation plan would be defeated by about ten to one ... and it was. Some snatches of memory flicker in my mind. There was the sympathetic smile of a veteran from the British Field Sports Society who told us that it took eleven years to win voting rights for their members. In fact we did win after four years of spattering blood on the carpets of Fishmongers' Hall, metaphorically speaking. I was watching greater battles for reform in other traditional institutions. Female priests were sermonising from pulpits in Anglican churches long before we understood that we were being blocked at every turn. Nothing I wrote to be published in the Association's literature was accepted. Invitations to demonstrate fly casting or fly dressing on the Association's stand at Game Fairs, they shrivelled up.

In desperation we did the unmentionable. We decided to 'go public'. I was instructed to publish a letter in our sport's popular monthly magazine, *Trout & Salmon*. The proverbial fertiliser hit the fan. Shock and Awe at Fishmongers' Hall! I had broken the gentlemanly code of *omerta*. It worked. Salvoes of supportive letters thundered through the letter box at headquarters. Phone lines were smoking. Branches were revolting. The Director was compelled to recommend to his superiors that they should appoint a working party to draw up a democratic constitution. There was a difference in the make-up of that working party. No more tweedy plus-fours and brandy noses in from the sticks. This time brains were imported from the city. I was invited to sit in. We produced a draft constitution. At last members would have the opportunity to choose and to vote. It was supported overwhelmingly at a special meeting of members.

I had a personal price to pay, as I knew I would. The persona non grata label would stick. I knew from the start that we could not win unless we pushed. As branch secretary I did the pushing. On being accused of ambition to win office I refused all such offers. I remembered the humourless gun-barrel eyes of those who dragged me down from the Labour Party's greasy pole of ambition. I remembered those militant apparatchiks from my short time in the crab-basket of Party politics; I realised then that if the militant apparatchiks ever gained the power of life and death as in the Soviet Union, I would become a 'wet-job', a price Hugh

Gaitskell paid years later after taking tea in the Kremlin. It was time for me to return to comforting obscurity in the shade of a willow tree by my favourite roach swim of the Medway at Tonbridge.

Years later, we game-fishing Men of Kent and Kentish Men met for our AGM in the pub at Goudhurst where Sassoon's Quorn met long ago.

We welcomed one of the reformists, the Chairman of the National S&TA, Tony Bird. He told us that had we failed to win our battle the Association would have lost its influence at Westminster. Government had decided that only organisations with democratic constitutions would be able to lobby in the corridors of power.

To commemorate what it had achieved, not only for our sport but also for the wider environment, the Association produced a sumptuous book. The doughty campaigners of the Kent branch were honoured with their well-deserved accolade, which I quote:

> *The reforms of 1994 did not go far enough for some members who felt that the management of the Association should be conducted on a completely democratic basis. Geoffrey Bucknall, the angling writer and stalwart of the Kent Branch was a persistent advocate for change. By 1997 he had convinced the Director, and yet another working party was set up, this time under the Chairmanship of Tony Bird. Their recommendations finally met the aspirations of those who had argued for radical change.*

The principle of 'one man, one vote' was institutionalised. How effectively it is to be applied only time can tell. The mechanism is there to be used. In the great scheme of things it is a relatively minor victory. Remember that old Russian truism, '"a fish rots from the head down." Bad things happen when good men do nothing.'

I was hoisted on my own petard when a coarse fishing club in Kent asked our branch to campaign against the pollution of the River Medway below Maidstone. Although we pointed out that our function was to support trout and salmon fishing, they pleaded that they had no voice to protect coarse fishing in the Weald and that a toxic estuary would kill migratory fish as well as coarse fish residents. They told us that they had fished a competition on the Lower Medway. The water was like treacle. We wrote a strong complaint to the Environmental Ministry.

Unknown to us, anglers had a representative on the Fishery Advisory Committee. He was incandescent. He wrote an incendiary reply to the effect that the campaign being fought by his colleagues had cleaned up the river so effectively that there were many coarse fish in the stretch. The anglers' lack of success was due to their own incompetence. He demanded an apology from us.

We discussed this at our own meeting. A member pointed out that as we had unwittingly insulted the river we should address our humble apology to the Medway. 'We cannot apologise to a river, can we?' I asked plaintively. We had in our ranks a classicist. He told us that in the old days it was routine to propitiate the River Gods. For example, one of them occupied the River Scamander which flowed past the walls of Troy. He kicked up hell's delight on Olympus as his sylvan stream was choked with the dead bodies of the heroes of the Trojan war. At last Zeus, Father of the Gods had to intervene to forbid personal duels being fought by the riverside.

'Surely those delicate river nymphs would not have had such powerful influence with Zeus?' I asked.

'You are mistaken. The River Gods are tall male figures with long hair and fierce horns on their brows. They joined battles on occasion. Scamander actually worsted Achilles in combat, trapping him in a net. If you offended a River God it was necessary to drive herds of oxen or sheep into the river to propitiate him, serious floods or drought might follow.'

'We can't round up the local farmers' livestock,' I protested. 'Isn't there a more reasonable offering we could make?'

'I think that as this is only minor offence a libation and a prayer would suffice to protect our fishing.'

'What does that involve?'

'I will write you a prayer to utter at the waterside. Then you must pour into the river your libation of some alcoholic beverage. Cheap plonk will not do. Only something like vintage wine from a good year will satisfy him.'

'I have a half bottle of Rémy Martin at home. That would even satisfy Zeus himself.'

It was agreed that I should take the prayer and the libation to the place where the match had been fished on the Lower River. Kneeling to ask forgiveness I would gently pour the nectar into the stream.

Creeping my way through the rushes and reeds I reached the river bank. Using one hand to extricate the stopper of my flask whilst fumbling with the document our classicist had prepared for me, I spilt some of the libation. My sluggish performance tested the patience of the River God so much that he directed at me a pungent cloud of raw sewage vapour. It overcame me. I could not speak. My eyes were streaming with tears. My chest tightened up. I began to choke uncontrollably. My only remedy was to thrust the mouth of the flask into my own mouth and to gulp down the rest of the famous nectar. In a few swallows it had all disappeared. Then dropping down onto all fours I managed to sneak away through the marginal reed beds before the God could discharge a second poisonous volley.[1]

---

[1] This is a true account of the letter I wrote to the Fishery Advisory Committee, though I received no appreciation of the goodwill of the Kent branch of the S&TA.

I did write to the Angling Politician with an explanation as to how we did our best to convey our apology to the river, but failed, forcing me to make medicinal use of the libation as an emergency measure for my survival. I gather he read this out to his colleagues at their committee meeting, so they would have understood that we did our best to placate the River God. My own reaction was that it was safer to stick to the local Anglican church, which put its faith in sacramental wine and after-service coffee.

*Good politics: N.W. Kent branch of the Fly Dressers Guild collecting funds for cancer research at the Annual Craft Fair at Penshurst Place.*

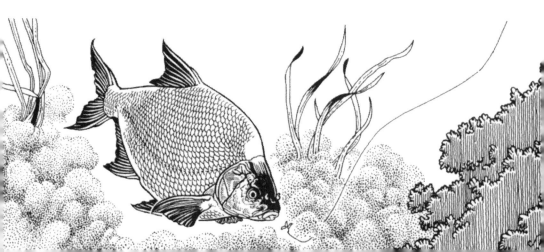

# 8

*Tonight the guns are thundering, and with each striking
hour bleached desolation creeps further through the land ...
and when the end comes – as come it will for some of us –
can we relive our golden days? Or have we grown too old
under the heel of might, inured to power, to speed, to all
things bludgeoned by materialism? Must we pass hence only
to leave this brazen god of ugliness triumphant?*

Romilly Fedden, B.E.F. France, *Golden Days* (1919)

AFTER *FISHING DAYS* was written I was invited to attend
a literary function in the City. I was approached by a
man holding a slim blue volume in his hand. He introduced
himself as a director of the publishing firm of A&C Black.
He told me how much he had enjoyed my book. He said,
'I would like to give you a copy of *Golden Days*. We
published this just after the Great War. I think you will find
that Romilly Fedden's philosophy is much like your own.' I
had no previous knowledge of this book, nor of its author.

I was bemused at first reading, for I was unaware of
any philosophy in my own writing. I had confessed it.
Fedden's book became my first love in angling literature,
the one I would take with me if Society were wise enough
to maroon me on that famous desert island. I did understand what the publisher meant. As I turned the pages I felt
a glow of sympathy and fellow feeling with the author.
'Philosophy' is too sophisticated a word. I think we shared
attitudes to Life.

Yes, we both loved France. His golden days in Brittany had
surely died after the slaughter in Picardy. He hated the
stupidity of military life though he volunteered to serve in

the trenches even at the age of forty, for he realised that there were greater evils abroad. On his reporting to his regiment, his Commanding Officer, who had learned of his artistic ability, set him to work to refurbish the battalion's drum. This made the point, didn't it?

We are unalike in many ways. He was tall and I am short. He was a gifted painter whereas I have no artistic talent at all. I believe we both shared a disrespect for Authority. And also for that other lower middle-class dictum of 'maintaining standards'; it is for the birds. Perhaps this is why I chose him as my fishing companion for that article I wrote for the *Fly Fishers' Journal*.

My time machine has its limitations. It will not take me to those streams of Brittany as it was after the turn of the century, and before Fedden saw the dawn breaking over gun flashes and the ambulances passing slowly through a blue mist. He hated the war so much that he said he had to do it.

Imagine a small town in Brittany before the Great War. A jolly party sets out in the Mayor's dogcart. The Mayor is a bubbly little man, forever rubbing his hands together in joyful anticipation of the fishing to come. The *Greffier* is the boon companion of the Mayor.[1] Then there is Jean-Pierre; what can I say of him? A Breton peasant with the fishing skills of a poacher, and an intelligent home-spun philosophy. He is always kind-hearted even when dead-drunk. As you would suspect, there is an unrecognised competitive spirit between them. Jean-Pierre and Romilly Fedden have a bond between them. If the word were not misunderstood and misused today I would believe that Fedden loved Jean-Pierre as a brother. They were both free spirits.

Fedden takes us into the grey *landes* beyond Republican France. There are hamlets too poor to boast a respectable *auberge*. There is a simple hostelry with a single bar-room for

---

[1] Greffier, a notary who is usually clerk to the court.

thirsty peasants. No inn-sign swings above the door to welcome strangers, but a bunch of mistletoe hangs there for thirsty peasants in the know. Against the wall is a faded sign which reads:

*Inn by permission of the King and*
*Parliament;*
*The Three Wise Men.*
*Dinner for foot travellers, four sols*
*Lodging for foot travellers, six sols*

On returning from the fishing you fear to meet the terrifying Gabino, a devil which, in the form of a great black-faced goat, haunts the banks of the River Arz at twilight. It drives unsuspecting strangers into the river to drown. The remedy is to grasp your rosary and loudly cry out: 'To hell, vile stinkard.' The Gabino will then utter a hoarse bleat and disappear. It never fails. I use it on canvassers at election times.

Yes, the rivers of Old Brittany were haunted by sprites like the Mary Morgan, who, according to Jean-Pierre, 'combs her green hair midst the reeds by the pool in the first blush of summer morning'. And the poulpiquets, who are only seen by moonlight in the remote parts of Brittany where tourists never venture.[2] But then do we not have our own headless black dog at Acle? Should you meet it by the river bridge your time has come, though you could try something like ... 'To hell, vile stinkard!' You never know your luck.

Jean-Pierre took childish delight in telling scary tales of the old devils of Brittany, such as the Ankou, a skeleton ghost which travels the *Chemins-creux* by night, riding in a cart drawn by four black horses. He comes to harvest the souls of those who have recently died. The Ankou profits

---

[2] Mary Morgans are sprites of the stream and poulpiquets are the husbands of fairies.

from technology as his skull spins on his shoulders, giving him all-round vision whilst skeletal assistants toss the souls into his cart. It is an occult form of refuse collection for which there is no charge on the ratepayers.

Jean-Pierre's other player when the wind was up the chimney on dark winter nights was the Loup-Garou. This was an apparently normal Breton peasant by day who was transformed into a slavering wolf by night. If you could draw blood from a Loup-Garou the spell would be broken. These weird beings roamed the *landes* as the black-velvet darkness of a Breton night descended, but strangely they also became hardened transatlantic travellers, dwelling amongst the French settlers in Vincennes, in Indiana, where they may have had to cope with street lighting, who knows?

However, having scared his listeners to death, Jean-Pierre would draw the sting, with a gentle smile, saying '*on dit ça ... mais ...*'

It is Cornwall that has an affinity with Brittany, and there, too, the undead beings have to be placated, for on the wall of my nursery my mother hung the Cornish Litany ... 'From Ghoulies and Ghosties and Long Leggety Beasties, and things which go bump in the middle of the night, Good Lord deliver us.' I have the modern version: 'no hawkers or canvassers'. And a Loup-Garou would have been rather rash to take on my English bull-terrier, 'Patch'.

Romilly Fedden survived the Great War. He died in 1939. His book is filled with the adventures of the four friends. An author's privilege, usually Fedden manages to 'wipe the eyes' of his companions, to choose one of those delightful phrases so beloved by angling scriveners of 'the golden age'. The shadows of war lengthened, Fedden and Jean-Pierre went their different ways. Fedden returned after the armistice. His book began with those stark words: 'Today I have fished again in France ...' But it was a different France in 1918; a different Brittany ...

When I read over and over again how the two friends left by

night in the dogcart to go to the station where the train will take them both to war, I am filled with an infinite sadness. The horse follows the ribbon of moonlit road, along the bank of the trout stream, past the white walls of the mill to an ancient chapel, dedicated to St Herbot. Fedden has painted here; it is close to his studio. They pause a while. But Fedden grows uneasy as he removes his hat to enter the chapel. Jean-Pierre reassures him: '*Ça fait rien, Monsieur. Le Bon Dieu n'est pas içi cette nuit. Il est au Kloar.*'

Fedden understands. It is the saint's day at Kloar, a nearby hamlet. The two men resume their journey. Each preoccupied with his own thoughts as the moonlight pours down on the ancient *landes*. Suddenly Jean-Pierre raises his whip to the sky, and cries out: 'I hate the Government. God how I hate them.'

That was four years before Fedden's return to France.

Jean-Pierre fell on the battlefield of Verdun with a German bullet through his head. Fedden closes his book with these words: 'I like to think that the good Saint Herbot spoke these words of comfort to the parting soul, not with a heavenly cadence but in a rough peasant's accent like Jean's own ... "*Ça fait rien; ça fait rien. Le Bon Dieu n'est pas içi cette nuit. Il est au Kloar.*"'

I wonder. Would there have been room for me in the Mayor's dogcart as they set off to the river? Would I have spotted Jean-Pierre's trick of winding a sliver of lead around Fedden's hook so that he could sink deeply his Invicta into the mill stream to catch the biggest trout of the day? So, when I had to choose a companion from angling's rich literature for the *Fly Fishers' Journal*, I went to my favourite book and its author. And d'ye know, I would have been at home there, by the hidden streams and between the bocage.

I have been amused by the foolish assumption made by some angling savants that the world would be a much happier place if all politicians became 'brothers of the angle'. This takes me to a schoolroom in the London Polytechnic where my wife and I had joined an experimental crash course to learn Russian. I recollect that we were subjected to some four hours' continuous bombardment with the Cyrillic alphabet and the mysteries of the soft-sign. I managed the first three hours splendidly, then just as my brain was beginning to flag there emerged through the door our portly tutor, Mr Pondorenko, who gave us a slightly sadistic smile and announced: 'Dictation!'

During translations from *Krokodil* I came across a story by a revolutionary soul who was sent to Siberia in Tsarist times. He was confined to a remote village through which winter rode his iron horse. The exiles had to survive by foraging. The writer noticed that one man excelled in fishing through holes in the ice and trapping animals. Even in the harshest times he enjoyed fresh meat, fish and furs for his body. He was in his element there. He was known then as 'Koba', but the world was later to recognise him as Stalin, described by his enemy, Trotsky, as 'the most bloodthirsty human tiger who ever stalked the earth'. At least he had one saving grace when in power, as visiting prominenties were installed in luxurious dachas, in the grounds of which were attractive lakes, complete with manicured 'swims' and ready-prepared tackle and bait laid out for use.

It would be superfluous to give you reams of statistics of the millions of his countrymen whom Stalin sent to their deaths. An example of that wonderfully ironic Russian humour of the times will serve. The family is woken in the early hours of the morning by a thunderous knocking on the door. An upper floor window slides open. A tremulous voice enquires: 'For God's sake, what's the matter?'

'Nothing to worry about, Comrade,' comes the reassuring answer. 'Your house is on fire!'

You could add a few names to the list of tyrannical angling despots ... Tito, or Franco, for example.

I have been reflecting on the two fly-fishing politicians in our own fair land. There was Viscount Grey of Fallodon. He was the Foreign Secretary who gazed over the darkening land when war was declared on Germany in 1914. He observed sadly: 'The lamps are going out all over Europe; we shall not see them lit again in our lifetime.'

Grey wrote one of the most famous books about our sport, simply entitled *Fly Fishing*. I was intrigued by his description of an angler's progress. In his early years he wants to catch the largest number of fish. He then graduates to the biggest fish. Last of all he revels in success against the most difficult fish, the ageing brownie under the brambles of the far bank, the trout which intends to die of old age. I would have added the final fourth requirement, that the place one fishes becomes more important than the captures. This is why I take my fly rod into the High Pennines, to the lonely vistas of Cow Green and Scarhouse reservoirs where the trout are eager, though small, and I miss their rises when my eyes stray to the cloud-shadows chasing each other across the purple fells.

Perhaps escape was in the mind of Neville Chamberlain when, having delivered his ultimatum to Hitler, he told reporters: 'I am now going to one of the remotest trout streams in the land.' I am less sure of the veracity of the tale that when a Foreign Office flunkey raced along the river bank to tell the Prime Minister that no reply had been received, he replied testily: 'Never mind about that now. Can you see what they are taking? I've been right through the box and cannot rise a damned thing.'

I thought that a profile of Neville Chamberlain would be an intriguing subject for my regular column in the *Fly Fishers' Journal*. I started the research with the popular image in mind, of the weak appeaser who gave way to Hitler in the vain hope of avoiding war. After all, Chamberlain grew up in the era when Field Marshal Haig told the Government that victory on the Somme depended on which gambler had the deepest pocket. The pocket, though, was to store the chips of flesh and blood. Memories common to many minds in the thirties were the mechanics of disarmament and appeasement. Today, when a politician launches an unwise foreign adventure he softens up public opinion by repeating the widely accepted legend of Chamberlain's Munich policy. It is a strange phenomenon, that an oft-repeated big lie becomes a truth to those who are too lazy or uninterested to search further. And had I not felt compelled to research my subject I, too, would have been in their company.

I discovered that when Chamberlain was Chancellor he negotiated the war loans which equipped the RAF with the Spitfire and Hurricane fighter planes which won the Battle of Britain. A childhood memory surfaced in my mind. My father had joined the RAF reserve. He was eager to take us to the airfield at Biggin Hill. I guess this was about 1937. I was enthralled at the Gloucester Gladiator biplanes drawn up in rows; shades of my hero, Biggles. My father poured a douche of cold water on my enthusiasm. 'They're obsolete. The German Messerschmitts would shoot them out of the sky in minutes.' And so they did in Norway.

It is true that Chamberlain tried to save the peace, yet he was not duped by Hitler and he worried that he would lose his struggle for peace, and with it his reputation. Later, in the Battle of Britain, when Churchill wished to continue the war against the opposition of a cabal in his cabinet, it was the single vote of Chamberlain that saved him from a humiliating surrender to Hitler.

Chamberlain said once that in war, no matter which side claims victory, all are losers. And unlike Churchill he had a more realistic view of what changes would be brought about by world war. He foresaw that the Britain's power and wealth would be exhausted and the Empire lost. This came to pass.

Chamberlain was a private man who could stroll through

St James's Park with his wife and scarcely a head turned in recognition, nary a bodyguard in sight. It is true that 'came the hour, came the man' when war arrived. That man was Churchill. When we visited his retreat at Chartwell I remarked to my wife, 'D'ye realise that had Chamberlain saved the peace we would be visiting a different house in a different part of the country?'

I found it hard to discover much about his fishing life. John Ashley Cooper gave me an insight in his fascinating book, *A Ring of Wessex Waters* (1986). He recorded the memories of Mr Percy Brown, river keeper on the Bisterne fishery of the Avon. It was Brown's job to ghillie for Neville Chamberlain who was then Prime Minister. You can imagine what an awesome prospect this was; fancy fluffing a stroke of the gaff to the PM's fish? Sir John Mills, the proprietor of the fishing, once asked of the ghillie, 'Do you remember when I made you gaff the first fish for the Prime Minister, as I was too nervous to do it?'

The nervousness was understandable, for Chamberlain had become a convert to Arthur Wood's revolutionary technique of greased line fishing with a light, single-handed rod and low-water style of fly. Blandishments were offered to the PM to change to an orthodox heavy double-hander, or even a spinning rod or prawn. Wood's ideas had not been acceptable on the Avon, it was still heavy-artillery country, but to their astonishment the PM succeeded in taking fish in his own way.

Anthony Crossley, a Member of Parliament at that time, became a convert to Wood's theories and published his own book on greased line fishing for salmon and sea trout. He explained that one hot summer when water was low he was persuaded to visit Arthur Wood at his home on the Royal Dee. On being ushered into the drawing room he was astonished and embarrassed to see Chamberlain ensconced in an armchair ... embarrassed because Crossley was an 'Edenite' who had opposed the PM's policy in the House. Luckily 'the brotherhood of the angle' took over, he was received courteously and soon both men were discussing how Wood's skimpily dressed low-water fly 'floated downstream like a dead thing' to tease stale fish in the warm water. The two men might have been at odds with each other in the House when Eden resigned as Foreign Secretary, but here they were '*les animaux de la même laine*' when it came to fishing greased line.

For myself, alas, the nearest I ever got to a fly-fishing Prime Minister was on being introduced at Fishmongers' Hall to Sir Alec Douglas-Home. I said to him, 'I suppose my invitation to fish the Hirsel is still in the post?' He gave me a sympathetic smile. 'I suppose it must be, Mr Bucknall.' As for poor Crossley, legend has it that just as the SS were dressing executed Polish prisoners in German Border Guard uniforms to fake the excuse for invasion, Crossley dashed back to Sweden to have one last fling on the magnificent sea-trout river, the Em. The plane crashed and he was killed.

I wonder why we perpetuate myths of famous men. Did King Alfred really burn the cakes? Was Neville Chamberlain the weak appeaser, an opinion nurtured by politicians for their own purposes? Did the Good Lord make us sheep so that we could be shorn? It is a good rule: never believe what you are told by priests and politicians. Ask yourself why they are presenting your lazy mind with a ready-made package of beliefs. There is no such thing as true history, merely massaged interpretations of it.

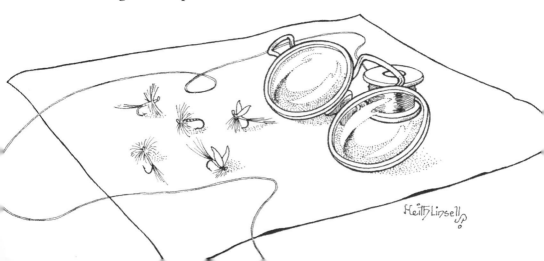

# 9

*Içi les larmes ne coulent pas ...*[1]
Jean-Paul Sartre, *Huis Clos*

ISUPPOSE IT IS Izaak Walton's description of our sport as 'the contemplative man's recreation' which preoccupies anglers with gloomy thoughts of the next world? Ghost stories abound, especially along lonely river banks at dusk. I was watching my pike float jigging along the far bank of the Medway near Yalding as the roach live-bait was doing its best to attract a pike, when my companion exclaimed, 'Come on, pack up. We've got to be off the river before dark.' I was startled; this was the witching hour when hungry pike left their quiet daytime lies to patrol the margins in search of prey. My friend looked about him in an anxious fashion, so I asked him the reason for his hurry. He told me that fishermen would hurry off the banks of the Medway at dusk for fear of meeting the little girl, bouncing along the bank in her Victorian dress. If she went past, the angler turned to watch her, but she was no longer there. The story is based on a cruel incident around the turn of the century.

There was a young woman, Hester Paye, who was scorned by her lover. She collected his daughter from her school in London, then took her to the station to catch a train to Paddock Wood. The girl was unconcerned as she knew that Hester's parents lived by the river, not far from Yalding. The woman and child set out to walk along the river bank to Nettlestead where her old folk lived. Their house is still there. En route Hester fortified her own courage with ardent

[1] Here no tears flow

spirits in the wayside pubs, treating the girl to lemonade and cake. She was remembered by witnesses. As dusk fell on a deserted part of the Medway she strangled the child. Fastening a piece of metal debris around its neck, she threw the body into the river. She did not realise that the Medway was in flood, so the body lodged between the weedy margin of the river and grass verge.

Hester went blithely on to spend the night with her parents. Unknown to her the body had been recovered and recognised. At Yalding an intelligent sergeant of the constabulary quickly understood what had happened. He arrested Hester who was subsequently arraigned for murder at the Old Bailey. To the amazement of all she was acquitted to disappear into the fog of history. The desolate shade of the girl is still seen by fishermen as she trips along the bridle path at twilight.

Salmon anglers have their fair share of unquiet spirits such as the unseen voice which shouts at the wading fisherman to leave the water immediately; this on a famous beat I will not name for fear of scaring you from it. I spent an uneasy night alone in a boat house by the Tweed where the upper floor was haunted by a young woman in grey. Seemingly, in less tolerant times, she hanged herself in her bedroom on being found to be pregnant, though unmarried. Visiting anglers are said to spend their nights downstairs, sleeping in armchairs and earning stiff necks for their fears.

I was tempted to meditate as to where famous anglers go after they have shuffled off this mortal coil. Waking from a dream, after musing on my subconscious mind's interpretation of Sartre's play *Huis Clos* (No Exit), I decided to capture the memory of it in the form of a short drama. Here it is, with apologies to Jean-Paul Sartre:

# The Fishing Hut

*The scene is a palatial fishing hut, like the famous gin-palace at Glentana on the Royal Dee. The impedimenta for salmon fishing is strewn about, rods, nets, gaffs etc. There are two armchairs, and a table with a fly-tying vice set-up, with various materials nearby. On the table is a bottle of malt whisky and two glasses. The door opens and a ghillie enters, accompanied by George Kelson. Both are dressed in the style of Victorian sporting gentlemen.*

GHILLIE: Here you are, Sir. Everything you need is to hand. If you care to glance out of the window you can see our trout stream. The salmon pools are further off.

KELSON [*strolling across to the window*]: By Jove, it looks just like the Houghton water. There's a fly fisherman down there, too, with his keeper. Pity I'm booked in for salmon, though.

GHILLIE: Ah, yes, Sir, I'm afraid that the trout fishing has been reserved for a Mr Castwell. You may know that he is an acquaintance of Mr Skues?

KELSON: I know Skues, of course. I suppose the rule is 'dry fly' only?

GHILLIE: Yes, quite true, Sir, the management here does have some strict rules to preserve the fishing. Our trout are very free rising.

KELSON: Oh, look. He's just hooked a good fish. I suppose the stream is well stocked?

GHILLIE: True, Sir, there are plenty of two-pounders. Now, if you'd like to make yourself at home, help yourself to a wee dram, I'll leave for a minute or two to find your companion.

KELSON: I didn't expect anything like this, you know. It's quite sumptuous. I suppose my name must be well known to the management?

GHILLIE: Have no doubts on that score, Sir. Your reputation precedes you. [*He leaves*]

[*Kelson goes across to the door and tries to open it but it seems to be stuck. He returns to the table and idly starts to sort through a few feathers. After a short space of time the ghillie returns with another elderly man in a Norfolk jacket.*]

GHILLIE: Here we are, Sir. This is the gentleman who will share your fishing hut. May I introduce you to Mr Alfred Jardine? He's best known for catching big pike, but he is also an accomplished fly fisherman. You can both make yourselves at home and get to know each other better. Believe me, you have plenty of time.

KELSON: Can I ask you, the door seems to stick, I couldn't open it? And I haven't a toothbrush.

GHILLIE: The management always seems to have trouble with the door. Sometimes it sticks and sometimes it doesn't. You needn't worry, though. When the time comes for the fishing, I'll come along to accompany you to your beat . . . as for the toothbrush, Sir, I can assure you, you will not need one here.

KELSON [*wandering to the window again*]: That's strange, that Castwell chap is still in the same place and he's landing another fish. Why doesn't he move on?

GHILLIE [*at the door, on the point of leaving*]: I did tell you, Sir, our fisheries are extremely well stocked, though some customers complain that the size of the fish doesn't alter much. I'm afraid that it's a strict rule of the fishery that you mustn't pass by a rising fish. You must cast to it first.

JARDINE: Well, that seems a reasonable rule, doesn't it?

KELSON: You know what anglers are! Some of them will complain about anything.

GHILLIE: Quite right, Sir, we do have our share of complaints. Now I'll leave you for a while. I'll return later to take you to your beats. You may care to make a fly or two. Thunder

& Lightning is popular here ... [*turning to Kelson*] ... of course, you know that fly, don't you?      [*He leaves*]

KELSON [*still by the window*]: Quite extraordinary. That man. He's still in exactly the same spot. He's just caught another fish ... He started to move off but the keeper pulled him back and pointed to another fish rising in the same place ... I'll go down and have a word with that keeper chappie. Doesn't seem to know his job. [*He tries the door, which doesn't budge.*] Well, I'll be damned!

JARDINE: I think you are, and so am I. I'm beginning to realise that this place is not what it appears to be. We may be here for eternity unless we can think of a way out. What do you suggest? Should we confess our sins?

KELSON: I can't believe that I'm a great sinner. If so, where are the bonfires and thumbscrews? Hang on, though. The ghillie did say my reputation was well known here. You know, there was that unfair accusation against me by Marston, editor of the *Fishing Gazette*. He accused me of stealing the credit from other people's ideas and inventions ... were they taken in by that, I wonder? When he mentioned the Thunder & Lightning fly he gave me a certain look. Was he making a point?

JARDINE: I remember that accusation. Marston really tore into you, didn't he? Page after page. Said you had copied lots of flies invented by others and then claimed them for yourself, your father and your friends. You said that Wright of Sprouston invented the 'Thunder & Lightning' when it was old Pat Hearns in Ireland. Now, if you confess we might both get out of here.

KELSON: Now, look here, Jardine, didn't Marston also publish that tale of the pike you landed at Amersham which mysteriously put on a few pounds after you caught it? The figure you wrote in the record book of the Piscatorial Society was a few pounds heavier than it was on the scales.

JARDINE: I estimated the weight it lost when drying out in the sun in the yard. I didn't know that someone else had weighed it first. Come on, have a drink, and then if we both confess to our misdemeanours I expect we shall be able to go to our beats. After all, they're always wittering on about mercy and forgiveness. I'd rather cast a fly for eternity than stay here. Time for us both to 'fess up.

KELSON: Oh, I suppose you're right. [*He picks up the bottle, examines the label and bursts out laughing*]

JARDINE: What's the joke?

KELSON: It's the Old Bushmills! Isn't that what you drank when the Mote Park fish broke you? And your artist friend told you to forget it?

JARDINE: I'll be damned. They must have a sense of humour up here. This was a satirical story which Francis Francis invented. It never happened. He wrote that I lost a huge pike. It broke my line and escaped with my terminal tackle. The fictional account became exaggerated as it passed from tongue to tongue. It placed me with the artist John Rolphe fishing at the Mote, near Maidstone. Rolphe invited me to forget it and swallow a few drams of the Old Bushmills as consolation. The story went on to allege that the keeper found the dead fish in the shallows with my line and bung still attached to it. He took it up to Marston's office in the City. Coincidentally, I was supposed to be with Marston when the fish arrived. I claimed the fish as my own capture. I had it mounted and displayed it at the Great Exhibition. None of this happened. It was a sick joke played by Francis Francis.

KELSON: There was another accusation in the *Fishing Gazette*. You knew that the Alexandra fly had been banned for trout stream fishing, yet Marston himself found you fishing with it on the Darent at Farningham. It so resembles a spinning lure that you may have been casting a fly-spoon.

JARDINE: I well remember that day. It had been raining cats and dogs. The river was still in flood. The water was cold and dirty. No natural flies were hatching. No other fly had a ghost of a chance in those conditions. I remind you that the fly was named after Princess Alexandra who fished the Darent at Dartford. The landlady of the Red Lion had prepared two ducklings for our lunch. I had brought a bottle of fine claret to share with my friends. That would have been wasted if we had given up fishing because of the high water.

KELSON: I also recollect that Marston wrote in the *FG* that you killed eight trout that day on a fly he considered to be a minnow imitation. What's your excuse?

JARDINE: I persuaded Marston to tie one onto his own cast, after which he was seen fishing down and across the stream, which is against the rules there. It must be the same gentleman's code here, 'upstream dry-fly only'. [*He nods at the window beyond which Mr. Castwell is seen still rooted to the same spot where he began fishing.*] That's small beer in comparison to a plagiarist like you, who hijacked other people's ideas.

KELSON: Let me tell you this. In a hundred years' time my book will be recognised as the classic authority on salmon flies. Marston's scribblings will have been forgotten in the dustbin of history. I didn't mean any harm. We stretched a point or two in claiming some flies for ourselves. But we improved them so we had a right to claim part-ownership. We just went a bit further in our enthusiasm. It doesn't seem to matter now I'm here. You know, it's really the fault of our competitors, pushing us too hard, trying to catch us out. Hell is other anglers!

[*The door suddenly swings open and the ghillie enters*]

GHILLIE: Gentlemen, the Management is keen to establish true records. The acoustics are excellent here. They hear everything. Given your corrections of slight errors of the past, I have permission to take you to your respective beats. If you would kindly collect the rods and gear and come with me. The river is in fine order for the fly, and you will find good runs of fresh fish. Your keeper is waiting.

Faithfully yours
Geo. M. Kelson

Oh, the same rule applies. When you catch a good one you must not move on if another fish shows in the same place. Trouble is that our fishing here is so heavenly; we have so much stock in our rivers that anglers actually complain that the fishing is too easy. Now, come along, there are two more anglers waiting to occupy this hut. I believe one of them used to own a fish and chip shop. He has booked our pike lake. I have to bring in some live-baits and pike tackle for him. The other is a competition fly fisherman. We do have a huge waiting list, you see.
[*The two anglers collect their gear and they leave the door wide open*]

I am aware that many readers will not know of our Victorian hero, George Kelson. They may be bemused to find him confined to a Sartrian *Huis Clos*. I regard him as a confidence trickster. In his time fly fishing was socially stratified. He operated in the upper social layers of society. He was a good psychologist. He exploited that feeling which we all feel on occasion, that failure is due to the wrong choice of fly rather than to an imperfect technique.

Sometimes I am asked who I believe to be the biggest fraudster in our sport. I have no hesitation in naming George M. Kelson, the so-called 'father of the salmon fly'. Kelson was a regular contributor to the columns of *the Fishing Gazette* during the last years of the nineteenth century. His reputation was made in salmon fishing, especially with the artificial fly. He won the respect of readers and the friendship of the editor, R. B. Marston. He depended on this relationship to pull off what was the most blatant hijacking of the inventions of other renowned salmon fishermen. His deception was on a grand scale.

In 1895 Kelson's book, *The Salmon Fly* was published. It was a sumptuous work. The colour pictures of numerous traditional patterns were depicted in a quality which owes nothing to modern technology. This established Kelson as the supreme authority on the subject. This book retains its place and price in angling's classic tradition. It also created the impression that unless a fly was dressed meticulously to Kelson's prescription, it would fail.

It is necessary to remind readers that in the glorious days of Empire, officers serving abroad were sending home exotic plumages which became standardised ingredients for the named patterns. For reasons which are hard to understand today, fly dressers developed a technique for building complex wings on their flies by marrying strips of various feathers, one on top of another. Relying on Kelson's authority it was accepted that such complicated fly patterns were *de rigueur.* It was like the absurd Victorian upper-class fetish of dressing for dinner even when no one else was invited. 'Keeping up standards' means institutionalising rituals which have no practical value. A vestigial feature today is the obligatory necktie which keeps you neither warm nor dry. Cast your eye along the sober-suited rows of MPs in the House of Commons. Would anyone dare to sit there with an open shirt-collar or a turtle-neck sweater? This was the ritualism to which Victorian salmon fly-fishers were conditioned by Kelson's authority.

Of course, it was to change when an intelligent angler like Murdoch proved that his invention, the Blue Charm could kill salmon even though the wing of this fly was a simple strip of bronze mallard flank feather ... but that was years ahead.

In retrospect we can discern that Kelson's scam was commercial. If a reader wished to kit himself out in the Kelson fashion he would travel all over Britain to buy his coat in one place, his boots in another. You may guess that Kelson earned commission on these sales.

The plagiarism of other anglers' fly inventions was on a massive scale. One day when I was fishing with dear old Jeff

Hearns on the River Moy he told me that his family still felt bitter at the way Kelson had lifted Pat Hearns' unique invention, the Thunder & Lightning, and credited it to his friend, G. S. Wright of Sprouston. For some strange reason other celebrities of the day were reluctant figuratively to challenge Kelson to pistols at dawn. One man kept his powder dry. This was R. B. Marston, who realised that Kelson's reputation had been made in the columns of the *Fishing Gazette* which he owned and edited. Marston waited for his opportunity, though even he did not realise that Kelson would supply it with a bizarre claim in his column in the *Fishing Gazette*.

Kelson claimed that salmon catches were falling because the fish were familiar with the standard fly patterns. You might as well dump your Jock Scott in the dustbin. However, he had the answer. He had invented a miracle fly called 'the Inky Boy'. Kelson addicts discovered that the essential plumage for this wonder-fly came from the tourocou crest obtainable only from a dealer in Paris. Those who took the trouble to dress the Inky Boy discovered that it was no miracle fly. Kelson replied that samples sent to him in the post were badly tied. 'Personally, I wouldn't dream of using any one of the samples sent which would make capital chub flies'. Marston added a gentle footnote that there was no reason why a salmon should refuse a fly simply because the dressing was slightly different.

In the New Year of 1908 Marston published a satirical cartoon about this controversy. Kelson was enraged. He could not ignore the snub.

'What in the name of Fortune can be the reason for throwing cold water on the infinitely more important measure of being careful and accurate in a fly to use when the most difficult conditions prevail . . .?' He also wondered why Marston had reviewed his book in 1895 only with faint praise. This was the opportunity Marston had waited for with patience. His reply was devastating.

"I hope I am correctly dressed at last!"

BLACK INK

A HAPPY NEW YEAR FROM INKY BOY

*This is the cartoon which was published in the* Fishing Gazette *at the turn of the year, 1907/8. Kelson claimed that salmon were refusing popular fly patterns. Familiarity was breeding their contempt. He forgot that you must have familiarity before you can breed anything. He claimed that his miracle invention, the Inky Boy would solve the problem. When readers complained that the miracle fly did not work he replied that the samples sent to him had not been dressed properly. This gave Marston, editor of the popular* Fishing Gazette, *the opportunity to provoke Kelson into the argument which caused Kelson to be unmasked as a fraudster and plagiarist. The evidence was overwhelming.*

'Kelson's book is supposed to give us the history of certain salmon flies. I say that some of these he claimed to have invented or named were neither invented nor named by him. Kelson claimed he was the inventor of making salmon flies with mixed wings. Salmon flies with mixed wings were made before he was ever heard of or thought of.'

Kelson blundered into the ambush. 'Name these flies,' he challenged.

Marston printed his reply in two columns over several pages. In one column was Kelson's claim of ownership. In the opposite column was the true origin of dozens of fly patterns. Many of the favourite flies of yesteryear are unknown to us today. You might think that that the Bonne Bouche is in the Michelin Guide rather than in a fishing book. Kelson plaintively accused Marston of being like the whale which invited Jonah to come in out of the wet, but his reputation was completely destroyed.

He owes his dubious rehabilitation to the fact that decades later writers and researchers found it convenient to have the dressings of historical salmon flies compiled into a single volume, a convenient directory. They had no need to go back to the true inventors like Ephemera or Paton. This is why Kelson, the great fraudster, is today recognised widely as 'the father of the salmon fly'.

When his book was reprinted recently I wrote a review for a fly fishing journal. I told the truth about Kelson. The editor asked me to withdraw my review. It seemed that another respected contributor had already written a laudatory review similar to those appearing in other magazines, all praising George Kelson's book to the skies. Editorial policy was geared to expediency rather than to integrity. I expect there were some dry chuckles seeping out of Kelson's tomb.

I am miffed about the 'Thunder & Lightning' fly, an Irish wonder which became a favourite of mine. Like the Silver Doctor and the Wilkinson, it was transferred to the Kelson

Mafia. Yet simply because of lazy and sloppy research a significant part of our sport's history has been expunged and replaced by a completely false legend. I hope that future angling historians will look up the *Fishing Gazette*s of 1907/8. They will discover irrefutable proof that Kelson was a liar and a cheat; his motivation was money.

I have met too many honest anglers who claim to have encountered ghosts to remain sceptical. I have had one experience myself, fortunately when with a witness, my wife. This was an audible ghost, like the Demon Drummer of Tedworth, an old soldier, who was never seen, but on receiving a command from a séance, it would tap out whatever rataplan was in favour to visitors in the Tudor manor.

This is what happened to us.

We had been staying at the renowned fishing hotel, the Red Lion at Bredwardine in the Welsh Marches, formerly famed for Wye salmon. Our companions there were dedicated barbel fishers. We were touring the ancient churches in the Wye valley when we happened on a lonely one which stood in the midst of a vast, open churchyard. Here was a long, gravel path leading up from the end of the village street to the porch. The entry was flagstoned. We had just entered the church, closing the door behind us, when my wife noticed that the parish register had been left on the table. Whilst she idly turned the pages we both heard footsteps crunching up the gravel path, then echoing loudly on the paving. Right up to the door. Clearly, they were female steps, for the sound was of the old-fashioned, unmistakeable flip-flops of a few years ago. I opened the door to let the visitor in, and to my astonished eyes, there was no one there, nor any other soul in the churchyard. I made a hurried circuit of the church exterior with no sign of any person at all.

I teased this out in my brain, for I had always been impressed by Professor Julian Huxley's assertion that 'all phenomena are explicable in naturalistic terms'.[2] Unlike Huxley, though, I do not discount an impersonal creative force within the Universe, for the alternative goes beyond the limits of human imagination. Whilst the scientific humanists are respected for being sceptical of classical Biblical miracle stories, surely, given relativity, quantum mechanics and thermodynamics you have three miracles to outclass turning water into wine? So, is there a rational explanation for ghost stories? Just as Paul Gallico found that the annual destruction by angry poltergeists of Lord Paradine's ancestral home was in reality caused by high spring tides in channels below the house tossing an entire wing into the air.[3] There seem to have been so many apparitions in Harry Price's Borley Rectory that they would have had to be on a work roster to avoid overcrowding.[4] Or the black-gowned nun would have been run over by the headless coachman and four.

I apologise for this diversion, but my excuse is that if Old Izaak was permitted to wander down theological byways in his angling tome, then I am allowed to follow his advice in using my angling expeditions as bedrocks for contemplation.

Even so, our superstitious fears can be exploited to win a favourite night-fishing swim which is occupied by a stranger. I recounted in *Fishing Days* how a latecomer to our carp lake at Wadhurst Park found that Trevor Housby, a respected angler, was ensconced in his swim, fishing over the other man's pre-baiting. Waiting until the surrounding woods were hidden in the gloaming, he coned a magazine to form a megaphone and proceeded to utter blood-curdling moans from the nearby chapel. Trevor, having grown up with the Cornish Litany, fled to the fishing hut where he locked himself in for the night, emerging in the bright light of morning to discover that his presumed swim had been

---

[2] See *The Humanist Frame*, Huxley and others, 1961
[3] Paul Gallico, Too Many Ghosts
[4] See his book *Poltergeist over England*, 1945

usurped by another who bore the ghost of a smug smile. And a sack filled with carp.

I came across another tale when researching the old and sere copies of the *Fishing Gazette*. Rarely nowadays do we hear the death-bell tolling for the soul of the departed. In our village long ago it was common for workers in the fields to doff their caps and count the distant clapper-strokes, one for each year of the life which had ended. The dear old journal recorded a century ago that a pike-fishing sexton was working in the basement of the church tower which bordered the River Bure. Anxious not to lose the chance of nobbling Mrs Esox while he worked, he threw out a bung and live-bait into the stream, attaching the hand-line to the bell rope. He was called away to other toil, forgetting what he had done. In the witching hours of the night the villagers were awaked by the tolling of the funeral bell. Hurrying to the church in their nightgowns and caps, they discovered that the sexton, in his absence, had caught a hefty pike which had gorged on the bait. In its struggles to escape the fate it had meted out to thousands of its subjects, it managed to turn over the bell . . . I wonder if they let the sexton keep the fish?

# 10

*And this our life exempt from public haunt*
*Finds tongues in trees, books in the running brooks,*
*Sermons in stones and good in everything.*
*I would not change it.*

William Shakespeare, *As You Like It*

I LOVE BOOKS. I am lucky to belong to a sport which arguably has the richest literature. I am also fortunate that one of my own books, *Fishing Days*, has become a minor angling classic. Some collectors list it amongst their ten favourite books.

There are two types of angling book. Those which are written to entertain are the least popular with publishers unless written by a media celebrity. I would not have found it easy to find a publisher for *Fishing Days* today. It is unfair to blame the publisher who has to satisfy the whims of the market place. Today the demand is for textbooks – where and how to fish.

This was brought home to me some years ago. A publisher of a coarse-fishing magazine discovered that the sales were falling because the articles he published were rather intellectual. He studied the market. He realised that the popular journals were those which published simple how-to-do-it articles with the minimum of text and the maximum of 'visual aids'. He changed completely the style of his magazine. In short, he 'dumbed it down'. I was one of the contributors whose writing was over the heads of the new generation of anglers. He prospered.

The writing was on the wall some years before. The East Midland Press decided to produce a magazine devoted to the popular specimen hunting. Their choice of Roy Eaton as editor was shrewd. Roy was definitely an angling intellectual. The standards he set for contributors were exacting. Specimen hunters loved this magazine, simply called *Fishing*. Unfortunately the publishers were not satisfied with a niche in the market place. Their business was mass circulation. They had misread the angling community. Advertising dwindled. Eventually they pulled the plug.

I have asked the captain of my time machine to drop me off at the Law Courts. It is a few years ago. I am appearing as an expert witness in a civil trial about patent and copyright. I recall that the defendant's barrister fell into the same trap when he put to me the most interesting question of this trial. He asked why the plaintiffs had protected inventions which had been described years before in angling journals. This was the occasion when I caused some consternation in the Court by unwittingly using the French word 'bricolage'. There was a deafening silence. Everyone stared at me. I explained that I did not know of an English word which had the same meaning as 'do-it-yourself' but with an experimental element involved. There are some terminal tackles which manufacturers cannot supply commercially because the angler has to make them for himself to suit his personal casting needs. The example I gave was the shooting heads made by fly fishermen for distance casting from the shores of big reservoirs like Grafham. Each shooting head had to be tailored in length and weight to suit the caster's fly rod and his ability to manage his fly line in the air. Another example was the shock-leader made up for a beach-caster to withstand the power being applied to the lay-back cast intended to deliver a lug-worm bait over a hundred yards from the shore into the sea. It would be some years before the 'trade' could supply efficient shelf-products to anglers who lacked the expertise to make their own terminal tackle at home.

I had a particular interest. I lacked the necessary physical strength to cope with the heavy and powerful tackle system for distance casting with the fly rods recommended by Tom Ivens in his book *Still Water Fly Fishing*. Tom was a strong man. He designed a mighty ten-foot rod in split cane. He called it his 'Iron Murderer'. I acquired one which nearly murdered me. It is beyond the scope of this book to dive into the technology of the sixties. Suffice it to say that I searched for a lighter tackle system which would give me adequate distance without exhaustion.

I discovered that bass fishermen in the Southern USA were using a scaled-down tournament shooting head system. After months of trial and error I discovered how to weigh out shooting heads on a chemical balance in the lab. The correct length and weight of shooting heads had to match my lightweight 8 ft 10 in 'Two Lakes' rod blank.

If you will allow me a toot on my own trumpet, by then I had become a director of a wholesale company, Sundridge Tackle Ltd. For a few years this 'Two Lakes' fly rod was the best seller in the UK, with a rewarding export market. The historical technology is described in two books I wrote.[1] The former book sold several thousand copies with a second edition and a further imprint.

There was a curious episode. The famous coarse-fishing columnist Richard Walker detested bank-fishing for trout on reservoirs, which he labelled in his *Angling Times* column as 'bone-headed athleticism'. Grafham reservoir opened on his doorstep. Over the newly flooded land the trout grew quickly and developed tremendous fighting power. Walker became a convert. He phoned me to ask about shooting heads and double-haul casting. We spoke for two hours. He explained that he was a martyr to sea sickness even on relatively calm water. He became an exponent of shooting

---

[1] *Fly-Fishing Tactics on Still Water* (Frederick Muller, 1966) and *Fly Fishing Tactics for Brown Trout* (Swanhill, 2000)

heads, so much so that his readers thought he had discovered them. When Barrie Rickards was writing Walker's biography he called on me. Brian was honest enough to put the record straight in his book,[2] page 183.

> *It is commonly held that Dick was involved in the invention of the shooting head and some have even suggested that Dick pinched the idea from someone else. In fact Geoffrey Bucknall introduced this idea from the USA where he had extensive game fishing contacts and he quickly passed it on to Dick and others for development in UK waters.*

I advised Barrie not to write the biography of Walker. I believed it could not be objective. His book confirmed my fears. It was far too laudatory. There were occasions when Walker lost an argument. They were omitted from the book. One defeat was in 1962 when he completely misunderstood the effects of a pike cull in Lake Windermere. There was a scientific account written by scientists Frost and Le Cren. After the pike cull the weight and condition of coarse fish improved. Walker assumed that this was because pike had been feeding on the best quality coarse fish. Either he did not know or did not take into account that at the same time literally tons of perch had been netted from the lake for an experiment to increase our food supply by canning them like sardines. Of course the remaining coarse fish shared a richer food supply.

Walker also wrongly believed the propaganda that the huge trout being stocked into small put-and-take fisheries were, to quote him, 'a new strain of super-trout making more efficient use of the existing food supply'. I asked him: if he found Billy Bunter scoffing cream buns in his larder, would Billy be a super-strain of human being making more efficient use of the existing food supply?

---

[3] Walker, *Biography of an Angling Legend* (Medlar Press Ltd, 2007)

I need this opportunity to correct one misunderstanding following Barrie Rickards' visit to me to collect material for his biography of Richard Walker. It is true that during the last months of his illness Walker wrote to me almost weekly. He also phoned me. Some of these conversations were so long that I heard his wife, Pat, calling him to end them as she feared they were tiring him out. It was common gossip in angling circles that Walker had a 'magic circle' of personal friends. I was not a member of it. I would describe our relationship as one of semi-detached friendship. I would put the blame on myself as I have always been slightly anti-social. I am not a people person. I was never close to him. We never fished together. I have never understood why he chose me to be a confidant, except perhaps that he knew that cancer research was my obsession. I collected and donated money from my talks and from my firm, Sundridge Tackle, sponsoring competitions. Amongst Walker's survivors I believe that his close friend Fred Buller knew and understood why Walker confided in me even though we were very different people.

I told Barrie that I had refused offers for Walker's letters. I had burned them as I believed they might hurt those who did not deserve to be hurt. I did not relate to Barrie the contents of these personal letters. He assumed they contained frank criticisms of other angling celebrities. This was not true. Fred Buller was right in saying that Walker did not attack other angling writers. I never heard Walker deliver a personal attack on another angler. He was perhaps the most tolerant writer I knew in a sport which is notorious for its bitter feuds: Halford versus Skues, Sawyer versus Kite, to mention two of many. I had no knowledge of the so-called feud between Venables and Walker. I doubt that this was caused by BV's jealousy. The BV I knew was a gentle soul. It must have been a deeper pain than that, about which I know nothing.

His letters to me contained here and there his opinions about life, with some personal experiences. They were not reprehensible. I thought that they should not be the subject of bar-room gossip in angling circles. They were personal and private. In one sense he was sympathising with problems of my own. He made me aware that he was far more sensitive than I had realised. I shall never reveal those private thoughts to anyone. That is why I burned his letters; quite a pile.

Long ago I was the target of another angling journalist. I had been invited to join a fishing party on a famous trout reservoir before the official opening day. After we finished a friend approached me. 'Did ye know that you were being spied on?' He went on to say that a scribe I had never met was crouching in the bushes behind me with a telescopic lens on his camera. A few weeks later there appeared in his column an article in which he told his readers that he detested angling hypocrites. He alleged that he had seen one such specimen at that Press Day. Although his target wrote authoritatively about fly casting his performance was lamentable. I burst out laughing.

'He is telling the truth,' I told my stupefied friends. 'This is what happened. A few days before that event I collected my first bi-focal spectacles. When you first wear them you have a job judging distances. I fell downstairs. My right wrist was so badly sprained that I couldn't even hold the newspaper. I nearly dropped out, but I was offered a lift. I could only cast and fish with my left hand. I managed such a clumsy short cast that I chose the dam wall with deep water in front. I made a pig's breakfast of my casting. That is what he saw. I owe him a drink as I was persuaded to practise casting with my left arm in time for my next eye-test.'

Such experiences are a warning to would-be angling writers. Even minor celebrities like me are targeted for malicious attacks. You may know the joke for amnesiacs, of a writer who on asking a beginner by the waterside, 'D'ye know who I am?' receives the response, 'Oh my dear chap, have you asked the Matron?' Rumour had it that I had conducted such a promotion for my book. In reality, I was at home with an active duodenal ulcer.

When Grafham Reservoir opened with fabulous trout fishing, boat hiring was rationed. You were allowed one or two hirings each month. There was a serpentine waiting list. The bailiff could be sweetened with an appropriate 'drink'. Citing examples of this corruption, a letter was duly published in *Trout & Salmon* magazine. For some reason the rumour spread that I was the author, using a pen-name. At a Game Fair one of those deprived of the 'bent' official's favours accosted me, challenging me to a fist fight, which I declined. Why was I elected to be 'the grass'? At that time I was the instructor of a fly-dressing adult evening class at the Hugh Myddelton School in the City. Unknown to me, my pupils had all signed a petition on behalf of the Bucknall class. It called for an end to corruption in boat bookings and for the guilty official to be sacked. It was dispatched to appropriate Authority. Both things came to pass. A KGB 'troika' court would recognise 'guilt by association'. In Britain, for the deprived beneficiaries it was more convenient to send me to Coventry than Siberia.

The editor of that magazine was a personal friend. I demanded to know who was the real author of that letter. After I gave him a promise not to reveal the name, he confessed that he wrote the letter himself. He could not allow his name or that of his magazine to expose some of his respected contributors who had greased the palm of the corrupt official. When I told him that I had narrowly avoided a brawl he roared with laughter. 'You've done a bit, haven't you, Geoff? I know your granddad was a trainer at the Thomas Becket pub in the old Kent Road. He was a titch like you.'

A book can be invaluable. Even if it only tells you 'two new things' it may revolutionise your fishing technique. This is how Lemon Grey's book *Torridge Fishery* improved my catches of peal during the black-velvet nights in the West Country. It must be admitted that the average angler has to have many frustrating nights in the river before he begins to score. When success comes, fishing in the dark for sea trout is arguably the most thrilling experience of our sport.

I must drum home again the dictum of Frost and Brown that trout recognise their food by its behaviour on or in the water. It is the age-old controversy, imitation or presentation? As a professional fly-dresser I was at first persuaded that exact imitation was the key to success. The Daddy Longlegs needed two knee joints in each leg. Those who teach master-classes in fly-dressing should recognise the error which Lemon Grey corrected in his book. The activity of the fly in the water is paramount. The fly should never be over-dressed. The hackle should be sparse and mobile to filter light. The wing should be slim and low. He tested his flies in the water to ensure that they would swim correctly. A badly tied wing would make the fly skew unnaturally. A bulky abdomen would spoil a quick, clean entry through the surface film. I was convinced; lesson number one.

Observation of his favourite Torridge made him sceptical of sea-trout folklore that after dark the fish drop down into the shallows of the tail of the pool. We chose our fishing stations accordingly, waiting until seven stars glowed in the firmament. We did catch fish. Lemon Grey argued that many peal went to the head of the pool, which was rarely fished at night. I described elsewhere how I made my best haul of sea trout on the River Ilen when a chilly upstream wind forced me to turn my back to it. I caught the fish with the hackled black-fly almost awash in the glints of the current coming down into the head of the pool.

Probably the most prolific angling writer was Alexander

Wanless. Ploughing through volume after turgid volume devoted to thread-line fishing in those days when the first fixed-spool reels would only cast ultra-fine lines with a breaking strain of two or three pounds, he drove home the lesson that hooked fish only fight against opposing pressure. By releasing the line from the pick-up Wanless was able to position himself downstream of lusty salmon and sea trout. He would ever-so-gently coax the head of the fish to turn downstream so that water entering its gills would kill the quarry. Reading the endless drab prose of Wanless was torture. I longed for the relief of one blinding flash of sheer mediocrity.

Yet proof of the Wanless pudding came to me when my friend Joe Tingle hooked a fresh-run salmon when we were fishing with ultra-light trout rods on the Teviot. I told Joe to slacken off the rod pressure. I crouched low-down into the water and I sank my net. Joe skilfully and gently guided the fish over the net and out it came. For the record, we were both fishing for trout with rods we built on blanks specially made to our requirements. Bruce & Walker gave us a parabolic action, loaded with AFTM lines, size 2 to 4. Joe's fly was a size 12 wet Blue Dun. We fished the Teviot every season up to the foot-and-mouth epidemic. Joe repeated this feat at the following year with a ten-pounder. Both salmon were returned safely to the water even though they spoiled the trout fishing for a short while.

The biggest fish I recognised as falling to the Wanless technique was a pike just a few ounces below the record. It was hooked by the Olympic javelin champion Clive Loveland. I met him at Knipton reservoir when we were pike fishing to raise funds for the ACA. It happened that he had a small pike as live-bait. The monster engulfed it. Clive remembered that I had described the Wanless pressure-free method of leading a big fish to the net. Bravely, he did just that. Out it came. For a few hours Clive would have held the UK pike record. The following day Horsey Mere yielded

121

Grendl's Mum, half a pound more. It was sad that dear old Omar missed the excitement. But getting astride my Velocette bike I tore up the A1 to meet Clive to verify his capture; it was one of the pleasures of pike ferreting before the *Fishing Gazette* bit the dust. Its ingenious editor, my friend David Carl Forbes died in a car crash shortly afterwards. The silver lining to that cloud was that the Pike Fishing Club was gestating quietly, waiting to be born. As Omar's successor I was a square peg in a round hole. I am not a single-species angler. I fitted my pike fishing days into a programme of trouting or getting salt spray from the ocean into my hair. Like another hero, Peter Butler, I too sat patiently on the concrete apron of a London reservoir, drearily hoping for the three-pound redfin.

So, I could list many books which guided my angling days. Space and time preclude me. This section is to prove to you the value of books which may have just one or two ideas to revolutionise your technique and tactics. The future of the traditional book is uncertain. We must fight to keep it. Please, do not buy books as antiques. Even the old classics have a message for you. Use them. That border fly fishing wizard, W. C. Stewart, with his advice to fish wet-flies upstream, seduced me away from the put-and-take fisheries on Southern chalk streams. A challenge from another century has brought my retirement home to Upper Teesdale. This is where the molecules of my ashes will return to the Universe which made them. That is eternal life.

You probably know about the American comedian who said that anyone who hated dogs and small boys was not all bad. My experience was different. I had been working hard in Korea. Having left an unpromising career as a laboratory technician with the Wellcome Research Foundation, I started my own business in fishing tackle. At first this business snowballed in the heady days of the seventies, but

*'Bringing up your son is the second hardest task in this world'...
especially if he catches bigger fish than you do ... Simon Bucknall
with a 22½ lb mirror carp from a lake near Sevenoaks in Kent.*

snowballs have a bad habit of rolling away downhill. My
partners and I had set up a modern production of fishing
rods in our factory. Then the cheaper ones arrived from East
of Suez. My colleagues dispatched me to Korea to set up
production there, for any attempt to match our production
to oriental prices would doom us to becoming patriotic
bankrupts.

Long plane flights, over the Pole from Paris, plus a dose of
jet-lag like malaria and I was ready for a holiday. Staying at
Hong Kong I noticed flights going to the island paradise of
Bali. I sent a telex to a hotel there, not realising that the
place was bereft of tourists due to a cholera epidemic. On
arriving at the airport I was chased up the road by some fifty
taxi drivers. The hotel was charming: a central block
surrounded by private chalets, each with its own pool under
palm trees. The chalets were empty of tourists.

By the light of a tropical moon I strolled down to the

beach. After a while I was accosted by a native who sidled up to me with the question: 'Mister, you want pretty Balinese girl?' I assured him that I did not. This puzzled him. 'Where you come from?' he asked. When I told him I lived near London, his face cleared. Realisation dawned. 'Ah, so sorry. You Englishman! You want small boy!' It seemed that some of our paedophile countrymen had established a reputation in Bali. I disabused him of this, and he left me in peace.

Yet he was right in a different way that night, for on meandering along the strand I did encounter a group of young lads who were making a poor fist of casting out a hand-line. So, I intervened to sort out a tangle that would have bemused Alexander the Great as when he was confronted with the Gordian knot. Eventually all was in order, the tangle was unravelled, the hook baited, and whirling round like a dervish, I sent it out into the deep.

Before long a serious twitching indicated interest. Bouncing through the surf, thrashing the sea to foam was a considerable moray eel. On unhooking this monster with due care I was astonished to see it wrap itself around a steel rod which was protruding through the sand. Such was its power and fury that it bent the rod into a loop. The children chattered with excitement. The fearsome brute was killed with blows from a rock and borne back in triumph along the beach to the lights of a shanty-town settlement at the far end.

I reflected that bringing up your son is the second hardest task in this world. The hardest is being that son you are bringing up. A fishing rod helps, but leave that to granddad. Visiting my granddad in suburbia, the morning was spent laboriously in cutting up the screw-on lids of my grandmother's food storage jars to make moulds for lead weights. In the afternoon we were both sitting on the ground by Keston Ponds. Then, as the sun was westering, he would haul a gold Hunter from his waistcoat pocket. 'Time to be off to the Fox,' he announced. 'I'll buy you a lemonade.'

The other problem for an angler is to decide to which social class he should choose to belong.

You see, fly fishing was traditionally the prerogative of the upper class, especially for salmon. Even when upper-class superfluous sons were sent by their superior families to earn their living with John Company, you would see, just before departure, the Victorian hallway packed with the impedimenta of a colonial sporting gentleman, the spears for pig-sticking, the rifle for potting tigers from the howdah of an elephant, and the specialised tackle Hardy supplied from Pall Mall for catching mahseer. This wasn't the true upper class of the man who would quit the high-summer dog days on the Itchen and Test to stalk deer in the Highlands and fish a double-hander on the Royal Dee. A grovelling ghillie was *de rigueur* for the upper-class angler. This humble being would have to acquire the appropriate vocabulary. 'Does the gentleman fish his reel on the left- or right-hand side?' The gentleman in question would always be addressed as 'Sir' even if an absent-minded Premier had omitted him from the Honours List. The ghillie would know his place. At lunch time he would remove himself from the superior company to munch his game pie and quaff his single malt at far remove.

No, our colonial was in a sub-section of the upper class. He would pass muster if he survived the rigours of cholera, malaria and too much chlorodyne. On returning from India he would be accepted with faint condescension. He would still commit the occasional faux pas like the ex-Indian lancer, Nolan, who offended the eye of Lord Cardigan by introducing a black bottle into the officers' mess. Happily this social misfit had his head blown off by a Russian cannon ball at the start of the charge of the Light Brigade. Much as you'd expect of him, what?

I have to remind you that the humble roach has been my favourite fish. I have admitted earlier in this book that my idea

*Early rays of the sun on Frittenden tench pond. Water provided by God. Rod from bamboo forest in Tonkin. Reel from British craftsmen long ago. Rod rest a present from woodland close by. Seating accommodation by Mother Earth. Valerie Bucknall watches her float at peace with the world before the Grey Men arrive with cement mixers and steel and souls of lead.*

of any reward in a second life would find me on the bank of a Wealden roach-pond in a pre-war landscape free from the sound of distant motorway traffic. Strangely, my father, who never fished, suggested at the breakfast table when I had just started to bring home roachlings for Pounce, our kitten, that fly fishing was the pinnacle of our sport. Pounce would snatch his prize. He would dash under the bed with it, from whence we could hear the crunching sound of fish-bones. In the pauses between mawfuls of fish dinner, we were warned to keep our distance by his low-key snarls.

A friend of my father had given him a trout fly to show me. Father believed that bread-paste fishing in the orchard ponds was the lowest level of our sport, fit only for peasants. He implanted in my schoolboy mind the ambition to raise my game when age and income allowed.

Today it is hard to visualise the class structure of fly fishing in Victorian and Edwardian times. It is true that there was a working-class tradition of wet-fly fishing in the North and in Wales. The dry-fly purism of Halford and his disciples was to separate the Southern chalk streams from this inferior paysan practice. It was much like the Gentlemen and Players structure in county cricket. Spectators noticed that participants emerging from the pavilion came out of separate dressing rooms even though they were members of the same team. Halford, though apparently no brilliant fly-caster, insisted that fly fishers on the River Test be obliged to cast their floating flies upstream. The easier practice, of chucking sub-surface flies downstream with the current, was strictly forbidden.

Cracks were beginning to appear in the fortress wall of class apartheid. The still-water Mecca of Blagdon opened for trout fishing a few years before the guns began to thunder in France. Even so, it was not the overstocked put-and-take fishery we know today. The annual stocking programme for those early years would be surpassed in a month today, the more so if big competitions were in the pipe line. My friend, the late Colonel Hatherel told me how the Army team stole a march on the Navy and Air Force to win an inter-Service contest by using a helicopter to spy on the places where the tame trout were being put into Bewl Water to sharpen up the needle match.

In earlier days writers like Bernard Venables described how hard it was to tempt the widely scattered fish. Authority even allowed anglers to spin with natural minnows. He told me that he knew of one fanatical angler who landed one or two of the line-sizzling trout. Being affluent, this fisherman bought a property close to the lake, only to fish on one blank day after another.

It was not the fishing which attracted me to Blagdon. The scenery was so spectacular that it distracted my attention when trout were rising to my fly. Blagdon brought fly-fishing democracy to Southerners. In the summer of the nineteen-fifties, my friend and I would leave London in the evening. We slept on a mattress in the back of his van. We fished from the first peep of dawn when poachers after wild-fowl were still active along the banks of the lake.

The relentless captain of my subconscious mind's time machine kicks me with two memories, one happy, the other tragic.

Before my first pilgrimage to the Mecca of Blagdon the victims to my fly rod from the River Teise in the Weald and Weirwood Reservoir over the Sussex border at Forest Row, none of them exceeded a pound in weight. There was no wind from the Mendips that morning. The meadow mist drifted across the surface, which was as calm as Mona Lisa's smile. At mid-morning a gentle ripple made Mona giggle, perhaps being tickled by the Lake Olive flies. Some ten yards in front of me a trout began to harvest these flies even though a noisy mechanical mower was giving the meadow grass a military back-and-sides. I tied on a winged Greenwell wet fly. It was taken eagerly. In those days, before the intensive over-stocking we experienced in recent years, the trout had full tails, not the eroded stumps where fish gnawed each other neurotically in overcrowded stews. My trout set off to the far bank like Phidippides in a hurry. I landed my first brown trout of some three-and-a-half pounds. Today that would be unremarkable. Then it was a great fish. I sent the Greenwell fly to my friend, Milton Tyler in Alabama. His nearest trout fishing was some 250 miles away in the Little Pigeon River of a neighbouring state. He sent me a photo of a fine striped bass he took on the same fly in the Cahaba river.

Here is the tragedy. Reservoirs are made by flooding land. The sunken features of that land remain invisible. They are lanes, ditches, hedgerows, tree-stumps and the like. Anglers know where these features are located. Obviously the lines of submerged lanes and ditches can be gauged from where they enter the water. As they attract fish the strategy is to position yourself so that you can safely cast your lures into the target area. But you must be careful to wade safely beyond the sudden drop in depth of the water.

After I had left my laboratory work I became self-employed. I had built up a small fly-dressing business which gave a modest, but sufficient income. I worked from home. A young couple called on me. Just married, they were having a fly-fishing honeymoon to fish on Blagdon and Chew reservoirs. They asked me to make some flies to collect on their return. They also asked me to indicate some promising places to fish from the bank of Chew reservoir, which I knew well.

I described a favourite place at Chew Lake where a ditch ran from the bank into the water. I drew a map. I warned them to stay well away from the line of the submerged ditch. Accordingly, I marked their safe wading positions with big crosses. I warned them not to go close to the sunken ditch in order to fish flies along it.

A few weeks after this they had not collected the flies I had made for them. I phoned the number they had given me. I was shaken and dumb-founded to learn from one of their mothers that they had both stumbled into the ditch and drowned. I believe the girl had tumbled in first and then her husband had gone in to save her, without success. Although I was shattered, I knew that I had explained emphatically the danger of wading too close to the ditch or to other sunken dangers. This is what happened; what more can I say?

Chew reservoir was new. Even so, such dangers of flooded land remain for decades after the inundation. Information at the fishing lodges warns anglers about these dangers. Even so, retrospectively I believe that an extra warning notice should have been displayed close to where they exist. In eagerness to gain that extra yard one can creep forward a foot or two closer to the danger zone.

Inexorably Time creeps forward. It is tempting for old-timers like me to bore the pants off the younger generation. If we were more sensitive we would notice their eyes glaze over when we start off with some time-honoured phrase such as 'in my young day . . .' I will be self-indulgent now.

What now starts me off? A customer came into my city shop. He was carrying a fishing rod which he uncased to display it to me. I cannot remember if the renowned Canon Greenwell was his grandfather or great grandfather. He bore the same Greenwell name. I was soon drooling over the Canon's famous trout rod.

Greenwell's name will always be remembered by trout fishermen, not only for the famous fly which bears his name, but also for the ginger hackle feather which had a black centre. These days there are fantastic capes, like Metz which are bred commercially. I suspect that the cockerels which bear them are as inedible as the beef from the Miura fighting bulls of Andalucia. India, too, specialises in providing almost everything needed by our Fly-dressing Guild members. You need a longer life and a longer memory to remember the frustrating post-war shortages of bicoloured hackles of stiff, bright quality for dry-flies. Fly dressers do not recognise the huge debt they owe to Peter Veniard whose expertise and quality control has sustained an age-old craft. Peter, in turn, depended on Jean Harris who had the keenest eye and experience for assessing the quality of dry-fly hackles. For keen fly dressers the post-war years were stressful. Food was so short that cocks and hens were never allowed enough time to grow a decent neckful of hackles. Things improved with time. I no longer helped the purist Teise farmer chase bantams round his yard so that we could pin one down with a forked stick to extract appropriate hackles from its squawking neck. Nor did I need again to cadge a filament of gold braid from the uniformed Commissionaire outside the Granada cinema in Maidstone where I went on Saturday mornings for the children's shows.

Sometimes we forget that when a North Country fisherman stipulated a coot's feather for the hackle or wing of his fly, it was because his twelve-bore had obliged him with that bird. We fastidious fly-makers would use no other feather. The inventor of that fly could have used a feather from jackdaw, waterhen, crow, or any other black-plumaged bird which bumped into No. 6 shot. The fish would not have noticed the difference. It was this streak of exigency in the nature of fly fishermen which Kelson exploited to his financial advantage.

This scion of the Greenwell family tree amused me by recalling the Canon's experience as a skilled salmon fly fisher. The manager of a legendary estate on the Tweed had always been reluctant to offer him a day's fishing. Seeing that the conditions were not propitious, one day he relented. Not only did the cleric make a great killing simply by offering the fish a smaller fly than was *de rigueur* on that beat, but he passed on this information to another angler who was not catching fish. This guest also started to reap a glittering harvest. Reports reached the laird's ears. He was displeased. The Canon was never invited back. He was fired.

Canon Greenwell's fly rod brought to mind the acrimonious controversy which occupied the columns of the *Fishing Gazette*. The argument was that the popular columnist G. E. M. Skues claimed that British fly-rods were far too heavy. Some of them even had steel centres. Skues had his rod made in America by the celebrated firm of Leonard. It was a feather-weight which he christened his WBR (World's Best Rod). You may imagine that the Hardy family was incensed. Skues was being unpatriotic.

It so happened that they had made a special rod to the requirements of Halford. It was fittingly called 'the Knock-about'. It was still popular in our post-war years. I owned one. Its weight and power knocked me about. When I studied the literature of Halford's time I understood why he needed such a rod. Apart from the steel centre, additional weight was added by a steel spear which tucked up inside the handle. Halford's friend and mentor Marryat fished with a rod over eleven feet in length. Marryat had a strange grip. He held the rod with forefinger pointing up the rod from its position on top of the butt. This is a weak grip.

One thing we do know about Halford's fly casting. He could not master adverse winds. With the puritanical rule for fishing upstream this must have been a hardship for him until Marryat showed him how to perform the 'storm' cast with which we are familiar today. Increasing the power of the rod gives no advantage to a fisherman who lacks the necessary expertise. It does explain why he asked Hardy to make such a rod as his Knockabout. We can also understand why Halford and Marryat had such a strong influence on British rod design. Given the propensity for hero worship in our sport, some deeper research may reveal that neither of them was a brilliant caster. That is the stuff of legend. Even by making concessions to the rod-making limitations of the day, on even terms I doubt that either of them could match the skill of a modern master like Charles Jardine, for example. This is heresy; I know!

Avoiding false modesty, where do I place myself in the fly-casting league table? I claim to be a good fly caster, but not equal to the champion tournament casters. I did win one tournament at a Game Fair in Denmark. I knew that there were two competitors I could not outdistance. Happily, the Weather God intervened on my behalf so that the managers had to re-arrange the competition in a sheltered area. It was based on accuracy, avoiding Khayyam's 'pitfall and gin'. My past experience on the 'River from Hell' (the local name for the Kentish Teise) favoured me against the Viking opposition which practised regularly from platforms facing the deep and broad lake.

I won by dropping my fly precisely into the hoops which had been secreted under trees, bushes, high banks, rush beds and so on. I made no libation to Zeus, the supreme Cloud Impeller, but the post-contest stress required medicinal Schnapps for me.

You may believe that I have been unjust to the fine rod-making tradition of Hardy Bros. This is not true. At that moment in time when modern man-made materials were still below a distant horizon, Hardy's produced a miracle rod in answer to the criticisms of Skues and his supporters. I believe it was the best fly rod ever made. This was long before Sundridge Tackle had started to manufacture my own 'Two Lakes' rod design in fibreglass. It explains the apparent contradiction that genial Jim Hardy awarded my son Simon and myself places on that firm's Roll of Honour. We both keep the official certificates for catching two hefty trout on the River Test at Bossington whilst using Hardy equipment. Simon caught a fish of just under 9 lb on a Spent Gnat. I had a smaller fish of nearly 6 lb on a dry Leckford Professor (Cow's Arse fly). Today those weights are not significant. In that time, though, they were outstanding.

I wish that time could be made to stand still before fibre-glass and carbon rods changed the fishing tackle trade. This Hardy rod design really was the WBR. It came to me at a time when I was deciding to buy my first 'real' fly rod. I believe it would have been in 1959. Before then I had scraped along with a much used, tatty Gold Medal rod with a pock-marked cork handle. In 1952, my mother and I had to buy a majestic Edwardian house. Her aged parents needed shelter and care. We converted part of the house into a granny flat.

I took on the mortgage payments, which ate up most of my income. Each week I put a little aside for my new fly rod. As a novice I needed advice. I phoned up Hardy's fly fishing instructor, Tommy Edwards. His own WBR was the JJH Triumph. He believed that it had the perfect taper for dry-fly fishing, yet it could propel a fly to about thirty yards across an adverse breeze.

The image of the Hardy shop in Pall Mall was of a posh frontage behind a stately Rolls-Royce. The picture gave me a feeling of inferiority. I had to pluck up courage even to walk down the hallowed Mall. The folk story was that King Hussein of Jordan was in the shop when it was crowded. He gave the staff a hand by demonstrating some of the rods to customers. To his wry amusement they believed that he was 'on the staff'. Those who know me will scarcely recognise the fearful young man crossing that holy portal with a flock of butterflies in his abdomen. That is how I felt.

Tremulously I asked the assistant to allow me to waggle the JJH Triumph rod. I did not like it. I understood why a brilliant tournament caster like Tommy Edwards would love its fast tip action. Its fast tip speed and narrow loop would have me unpicking wind-knots in the leaders. I asked if there was a lighter rod with a more supple action. When he put the CC de France nine-footer into my hand I knew instinctively that this was the rod for me. I fished with it year by year, even well past the time when the miracle of carbon fibre expedited split cane into the museums. I understand from those monomaniacs who collect classical tackle for their display cabinets that it is the most-sought split cane fly rod.

There is a half-way house for senior citizens who love traditional items of fishing tackle, not to be displayed for

*Geoffrey claims that the CC de France nine-foot fly rod built in split cane by Hardy was the perfect tool for fishing still-water for trout. It was Hardy's answer to the long and sometimes bitter campaign by Skues for traditional British fly rods to be lighter. Geoffrey regrets that modern man-made materials like glass and carbon fibre brought about the end of the era of true craftsmanship in rod building. This picture shows his own rod and his capture of a fine Blagdon brown trout on a Greenwell Glory in the post-war years before the intensive stocking we know today.*

adoration, but to be used. If that sympathetic angel confines me to a Wealden roach pond for eternity, I trust he will let me bring my favourite Ariel centre-pin reel. After all, angels are human, aren't they? I believe it was St Michael who had to bear a message to the wine cellars of Haut-Brion. When he failed to return a teetotal guardian angel was sent to escort him back to Heaven. He was found on the floor in the cellars, blissfully asleep, with a beatific smile on his lips; but he was pissed as a newt.

As professional teachers my parents settled comfortably into the middle class. When I became a fishing tackle retailer, Napoleon instantly recognised me as a shopkeeper, so I was demoted to the lower middle class, the home of those 'in trade'. As I fished for roach, this was appropriate. Eyebrows were lifted when I was recognised as a dry-fly man. I had ideas above my station. Then, when the recession put me out of business and on to the dole I was perplexed as to which class I should join. The problem was solved on reading Turgenev. I recognised myself and I was accepted into the ranks of his 'lower dregs'. I was there until the Civil Service granted me enough redundancy money to set up an office at home where I could write. I found myself in the new category founded by John Major, the working poor. I have been there ever since. I was glad to leave the lower dregs. The lower dregs class is not comfortable, for no matter how low a man sinks, he can always find comfort as long as there is someone below on whom he can look down. There is no one below the lower dregs.

Long ago each class had its appropriate angling label. In recent years the borders began to erode. Working-class men threw flies across their rain-fed streams in the North. Some toffs were seen spinning for pike, a coarse fish. After the war Suburban Man found his local reservoir offered trout fishing under a fly-only rule (now abandoned). The whole system became a mess. Even the brown-booted parvenu was seen on Highland salmon rivers. And by making a generous donation to Party funds, a successful parvenu can buy into the House of Lords, and if he doesn't drop too many aitches, he may be invited to throw a salmon fly into the Royal Dee ... after all, there is more room there now that traditional salmon fishers go to Russia where mosquitoes and easy salmon abound. Happily, the Gulags where Beria housed his 'counters' are now converted into comfortable fishing hostelries.[3]

---

[3] 'Counter' in Russian was NKVD slang for 'counter-revolutionary'.

# 11

*You could not step twice into the same river, for other
waters are ever flowing on to you.*

Heraclitus

HERE YOU ARE, I am in danger of becoming enmeshed in
philosophy, for was not that famous Greek sage from
Ephesus trying to convert me to his belief that Life is always
in a state of flux? Or should I, metaphorically speaking, be
like Hermann Goering, reaching for my pistol when I hear
the word 'intellectual'? I should have listened to Heraclitus,
for when the opportunity came for me to take a rod on the
River Test at Bossington I fondly imagined that the river
flowed as much as it did when Halford sadly closed the
wicket gate behind him after his Houghton Club lost the
fishing rights there.

Why was I offered a rod when it was said that even God
would have been put on a waiting list? I'm not sure; my
memory fails. Was it because I casually let it become known
that my father was an expert in Spitfire engineering in the
RAF during the war, for not many realise that the factories
delivered some of the planes in kit form? The Air Force had
experience in cannibalising wrecks and rebuilding damaged
planes during the Battle of Britain. My father involved
himself in Spitfire assembly in South Africa; on completion,
he had them flown up to the Desert War via Kenya where he
slept at night with a cocoa-tin and pebble balanced on his
bedroom door handle and a loaded revolver under his
pillow.

Our side of the river at Bossington was Spitfire country,
the Fairey family owning the estate. Our rivals on the far

bank were Hurricane men, for there Tommy Sopwith's guests tossed their dry flies. The point was made when our landlord barrelled his personal Spitfire low over the river just as I was putting a Blue-winged Olive to a reluctant trout. I was an unwitting dry-fly purist thanks to my farmer-mentor on the River Teise in the Weald. Naturally my reading was of Halford and Marryat in days of yore when the water meadows were flooded, the river so filled with wild brown trout that in 1842, Lord Glentworth, renting a nearby cottage, wrote in his diary to commemorate his last day there: '*Sent Charles out with the shoe net in the morning as I wanted fish to take away. He brought thirty three, all good fish, one of 1lb. We packed them all up, got into our gig and adieu to Longparish. Sorry to go.*'

The noble Lord kept a record of his catches in 1842. He fished for seventy-five days and averaged over thirty-six trout each day. Did he, I wonder, like the sporting Colonel Hawker, fish from horseback? Or did he fish the cross-line on windy days? I leave to your imagination whether or not this was a two-man operation, one on each bank with a fly-laden line between them.

Although the upstream cast was *de rigueur* the purism of Halford had long since bitten the dust. I was dismayed to learn that nymphs were permitted in the dog days of summer. My protest at the Syndicate meetings was of no avail. Nor did I relish the introduction of semi-tame rainbow trout, weak-minded fish which were so brainwashed by regular arrivals of trout pellets in the stews that they came up to all floating debris, from grass seed to fag ends. Indeed, copies were made by inventive minds, the Pelletus fly and the Fagendus floater.

Even so, one day I knew that the eagle eye of a neighbouring fisherwoman had imagined that I was fishing downstream, so I had to hurry to warn the bailiff. She had not realised that I was facing downstream on a weir to *fish upstream* along a strong back current. She went to the keeper 'to grass me up'. I was pleased to learn that she had been shot down in flames, so to speak.

This was the end of innocence. For a fly fisherman to fish the River Test was akin to a club cricketer being invited to play at Lord's. I had a vague idea that the river was stocked. I did not know that replacement of fish caught was on such a regular basis that one day I was fishing at one end of a beat when the bailiff was tipping rainbow trout into the water at the far end. What was the shelf-life of a stocked fish? Barely a few days, perhaps even hours.

It was not like that at first. Our keeper was Reg Dade, but, anticipating retirement, he was criticised by some anglers for neglecting the fishery. This was brought home to me when my leg fell through a rotten plank on a footbridge, necessitating the humiliating 'fireman's lift' to the hut from a colleague, followed by hours of painful surgery to a burst blood vessel. Even so, on balance I preferred the wild state of the fishery. It was like a fading Victorian roué. The bank-side grass was uncut. You could not creep through the morning dew in slippers. The trees behind the margins were not hacked away to spare the careless back-cast from entanglement. As another friend once remarked to me: 'The difference between a bad caster and a good one is that the bad one hooks the lower branches and the good one hooks the upper branches ...' and after a moment's reflection, he added, 'The bad caster recovers his flies, though, and the good caster loses his.'

Having been brought up on the tangled Wealden Teise, nicknamed by some frustrated casters as 'the River from Hell', I relished the careworn stream. It still presented problems. It was amusing to see a worn patch on the bank where every fisherman had stood to throw a fly at the same visible fish under the far bank. I could understand why it had survived this bombardment ... in a word, 'drag'. There was a savage eddy above the fish. Being ambidextrous, I was able to change the angle of attack with a left-handed throw.

Thus it was during the last days of Reg Dade, who was ever kind to me, so much so that I attempted in vain to fill his hollow legs with Scotch in the Boot Inn. When he retired the new regime took over, and why should I criticise? It gave the fee-paying members what they wanted: manicured trees, savage weed-cuts, grass margins like cricket pitches, ever-eager rainbows fresh from the stews. No. I dare not criticise. Fisheries are in the estate's market place. Management needs must give its members what they desire, easy fishing for easy fish. After all, I had an option, to take my jaded appetite elsewhere. In my days of innocence I had imagined that the chalk streams would be as I found them in the books of the Golden Age. Realisation dawned as to why Skues of old stalked off the Itchen in fury when the modern age of fly fishing dawned. If dear old Reg had condemned me to agonising times when I clung to the bars of a hospital bed whilst a sadistic surgeon stuffed my weeping haemo-toma with wads of gauze, I still thanked him for giving me a year or two by the River Test much as it must have been when Halford and Marryat were bickering in the nearby Mill because 'F. M.' had forgotten to put the body-straw for mayflies in to soak the night before.

The crunch came to me like that uproar of the butterfly's wings in the neighbouring meadow which disturbed Wode-house's afternoon nap whilst it sparked off an earthquake on the far side of the Globe. I was resting by the bridge, my net carelessly discarded nearby, when a baby stoat tripped over the planking and fell into its mesh. Its button-bright eyes stared into mine, those of a fellow predator. I was entranced by its fiery-brown jacket and ivory-white shirt-front. Stoats are always dressed for dinner. I carefully disentangled it and let it go. A furious keeper berated me. Stoats were the enemy of Game. I reflected he must have been a member of the gallows old-school who had never read Vesey-Fitzgerald's assessment[1] that many of the supposed enemies of Game do less harm than good. It was a small world in some ways, locked into a time warp where voles were exterminated, yet conceding to the modern demand for 'put-and-take' fishing.

You know, there were still times, perhaps when the dusk was beginning to obscure the far bank and the wisps of smoky mist were seeping from the meadows, when I would fish the Test with half-closed eyes, seeing it as if a century had never passed me by. That was a time when the sherry spinner was on the water with fish, losing all caution, slashing at them wildly, making those turbulent kidney-shaped whorls. Every imitation would be refused, yet a natural fly close to my own copy would be engulfed. Every tame rainbow trout had become as fastidious as an old survivor, whilst I would frantically 'go through the fly box' to find the answer.

Then my friend, John Spurway, relaxing on the riverside bench as the evening rise died away, there would he see through the gloaming drovers with their cattle crossing the ancient ford whilst chattering to each other in a language that sounded like Welsh. There were no such cattle and drovers nearby. In the magic of that mystery between day and night, Time had lifted its veil to show him a glimpse of those who once crossed this river centuries before, to take their herd to an old earth-fort on a distant hill. Then night closed down the shutter and John was again locked into the mist swirling off the meadow.

I remain grateful to my chalk stream days. I fished the Itchen and Anton, sometimes catching a glimpse of my snow-haired hero, Bernard Venables, stalking a rise on the far bank. The Grey Men with their concrete mixers despoiled the Itchen where I fished. The Wylie had chosen

---

[1] *British Game* in the Collins New Naturalist series.

to run between two busy roads and a railway line; you did not need to take your tinnitus with you, it was waiting for you there. By the Test, at dusk I could still see a ghostly barn owl quartering the meadows between the river and the busy traffic queues choking the road beyond. There came a time to move on, to find a greater challenge, a wilderness where the hand of God put the trout into the rivers. The books of Halford and Skues were left unopened on the shelves and my questing hands reached up for Stewart and Pritt. True, that dedicated Southerner Hilaire Belloc only saw the Northmen for a day; that was enough for him, but I was hypnotised by their fast streams and, hopefully, truly wild trout. There came a time to move on, to find a greater challenge, Lavengro's 'wind on the heath, brother. Two good things.'

Fly fishing is like many other human activities. It reaches a classical period which is challenged by iconoclasts, after which it slips into decline through popularity. I experienced two examples of this.

The first was in bullfighting. I am no taurophile, but whilst in Spain in the fifties I stayed with a tailor who was a dedicated *aficionado de toros.* I had to swallow whatever reservations I had, so whilst being conducted to the Plaza de Toros of a Sunday I adopted the wise disguise of Isherwood in pre-war Nazified Berlin. Like him, I became a camera, recording and remaining silent.

Now, bullfighting had its classical golden age when traditionalists like the renowned matador Manolete performed elegant *verónicas* with their fighting capes. Not for nothing did the Spanish novelist Ibañez describe the crowd in the bullring as 'the Big Animal', for the swordsman was urged to take bigger and bigger risks. This culminated in many new passes, such as *'el telefono'* when the matador kneeled in front of the savage beast, leaning his elbow on its blood-bedewed head to imitate someone speaking on the phone.

In 1936, a tired and overweight matador, Sanchez Mejías, teased one of the mighty bulls from Guisando, a beast called 'Granadino'. Mejías sat at the foot of the barrier to make his '*faena*' with no space to move away from the horns. The bull nailed his thigh, and, Mejías being carried under the hot sun to distant Madrid, the eggs of gangrene hatched in the wound; he died. His lover, the poet Lorca, wrote his lament, one of the most recited poems in the Spanish language. The opening words: '*A las cinco de la tarde*' were repeated like the hammer blows of fate.[2] This was the result of the businessmen titillating the appetites of the Great Unwashed in the cheap seats.

Nearer to home there is the 'popularisation' of our national sport, cricket. Those of us who relished its golden age bestow a sardonic smile on the batsman accoutred in colourful pyjamas and body armour, unrecognisable under his hauberk, as he waddles like a pregnant duck to the crease. I sit in the stand at the Oval and close my eyes to revisit the time when I saw Jim Laker spin out all ten Australian wickets on uncovered green grass. I know that Tony Lock once told me that there were not enough 'sticky dogs' for him that season, but would he not have smiled at the tale of the millionaire who bought his son the MCC for a Christmas present when the lad begged Santa for a cowboy outfit?

So it was with dry fly fishing on chalk streams like the Test.

There was a golden age, at its pinnacle just before the Great War. We salivate when we read of it in the classic tomes by Halford. The first challenge came from Skues himself when he introduced nymphs on to his Itchen water. He was right. It did make fishing easier. That was not the point. Consciously or not, the art which had evolved, probably by

---

[2] 'At five in the afternoon'.

accident, was to overcome the instinctive caution of the trout by skill. The traditional rules were framed to preserve that skill, but gradually pressures were exerted. As fisheries became competitive with each other the rules were relaxed. The fly was allowed to sink, and might it not be moved in a subtle fashion, eventually like Oliver Kite's 'induced take' with a bare hook? Artificial stocking was introduced. Skues hated it. And what would he have said to the rainbow-hued interlopers from abroad, I wonder? It became almost a free-for-all, ultimately described as 'put-and-take' fishing. The giants of old, Marryat and Halford, would not recognise it.

There, one day John Goddard was my guest on the Test. I knew he preferred to fish 'no kill'. I was gobsmacked when I saw him coming back down the river with two dead rainbow trout in his hands. 'These buggers are best out of the water!' Did he say that to me? Anyway, he ought to have said it.

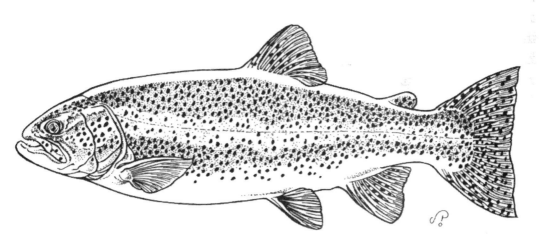

# 12

*Those who obstinately oppose the most widely held opinions more often do so because of pride than lack of intelligence. They find the best places already taken and they do not want to take the back seats.*

La Rochefoucauld, Maxims

O F COURSE, THOSE cynical words by La Rochefoucauld could equally be applied to the traditionalist as well as the iconoclast . . . when I was turning those sere pages of the *Fishing Gazette*s I came across the great feuds and vendettas of long ago. I knew from my own short foray into politics that the ideological differences inevitably devolved into clashes of personality. How else can they be expressed?

The first verbal duel was instigated by the traditionalists who, around the end of the nineteenth century, favoured the braided horsehair leaders and resisted the new-fangled silk-worm catgut. They fought a doughty rearguard action. One of their champions entered the lists, challenging the editor of the *Fishing Gazette*, R. B. Marston, to a joust on the Yorkshire trout streams. This warrior was Robert Balderstone who wrote under the pen-name of 'Herne the Hunter'.

Marston was to use gut leaders, Balderstone to use horsehair. Marston won hands down, so inevitably his rival accused him of cheating! Marston riposted that Balderstone was 'no gentleman', and in those days that was an insult supreme.

It follows that commercial considerations were intertwined with these ancient fly-casting contests of yesteryear. In those days of mutton-chop whiskers the House of Hardy swept up the trophies, thanks to their own champion, J. J. Hardy. The rods were splendid double-handed miracles of split cane. Then there emerged from the mists over the Irish bogs a formidable opponent bearing the ancient and old-fashioned weapon of Greenheart, with its taped-up spliced joints. John Enright was a brilliant caster. He outdistanced everyone until Mr Hardy hit on the stratagem of having the old Greenheart rod disqualified by a technicality. Poor Enright could not perform so well with a borrowed rod.

Yet he knew a trick or two, and on creeping around the tents where was kept the Hardy armoury he found that his opponent had fastened a button to the end of his rod (though what advantage this gave, I know not). Tragically John Enright died young and Hardy gave a generous tribute to his memory.

There was no such chivalry when Skues, at the height of his popularity, praised the lightweight trout fly-rods built by Leonard in America. The Leonard rod was a marvel, a swan feather in split cane. Skues compared it favourably to the designs which Halford had in mind for Hardy, a powerhouse to put a dry fly upstream into a boisterous breeze on the Test. Skues had his partisans, though the traditionalists unhorsed him in the lists. Skues had bravely taken on the British rod-making industry, and he lost.

My own business career in the fishing tackle trade has an oblique bearing on this old brouhaha about ultra-light fly rods. This book is not about my commercial life. Briefly, my colleagues and I had built up a large wholesale and manufacturing business. After a few years I discovered, in a moment of enlightenment underneath a palm tree on a moonlit beach of a tropical island, that I was no businessman. So, asking my partners to buy me out, I spent a few enjoyable years discussing fishing from behind the counter of my City tackle shop. It was at this time that, having over-indulged myself on the banks of the Test, I had an attack of tennis elbow which put me on the rack. My assistant, the brilliant fly dresser Annie Douglas, suggested that I could still waft out a fly with a short and slim fly rod we had unsold, a marvel that was confected to throw a size 2 line.

Although I once failed to stop a runaway trout from ploughing through three weed beds, the rod was a delight ... if only it were longer, I sighed when the pain yielded at last to the gimlet fingers of the osteopath. I scoured the trade catalogues. No such thing was made. 'Why not have one made for you?' counselled Annie.

There followed phone calls to the blank-makers. Ever a hero-worshipper, I was besotted with Charles Ritz and I wanted his so-called 'parabolic' action in the rod. I think he invented this term for a rod action which had a fast-tip for line speed, though when a fish was hooked, the shock-absorber effect would come down through the whole rod. A fish could not break free on fine leaders. Like Skues of old, his rod designs and casting ideas were light years ahead of his time, so they were treated with derision by the Establishment. Indeed, at a Game Fair, when asked to perform on the platform, seeking the rods made for him by Pezon & Michel, he came into the marquee, crowded with the good and the great, and plaintively enquired, 'Has anyone seen my pair of Parabolics?' This innocent plea for help brought the house down. Jacques Michel, knowing I was a Ritz fan, bestowed on me one of his 'Fario Club' split-cane rods, though it was only some eight feet in length. I wanted a longer rod to be made for me in the new carbon material. I had in mind Stewart's advice for upstream work, 'long rod and short line'. At that time the northern streams were being plundered of their water, showing their bare bones, due to a drought. Finesse was called for to avoid spooking the fish. Everything came together. Two firms succeeded in making exactly what I wanted. The first one was Harrison, of Liverpool, but my small-scale needs were not fitted to his production. Then, some nine months of toing and froing to Huntingdon brought about my ideal from the rolling tables of Bruce & Walker.

This short digression into commerce is to set the scene for my dilemma. I thought I had a revolution in my pocket, but did I have the stamina to take on the might of the fishing tackle trade as well as the traditional 'heavy line' ranks of the British fly fishers? I recollected the storms around the head of Skues. He relished them. I did not. I remained content with converting a small number of connoisseurs who came to my City shop; perhaps about a hundred in all.

I described the technical details in my last textbook, *Fly Fishing Tactics for Brown Trout*. I did some modest evangelising to put to bed the fears of those who thought a light line would blow about in the wind. On the Wharfe I demonstrated how the fine line would cut through the wind because of its lower resistance. I showed the watchers how I could put out a long line with the speedier rod tip. Then one day I was asked to provide rods to be tested by two angling writers of renown, who professed to have been searching for such qualities for years. I was asked within a week or two to collect the rods. 'They don't load up on the back cast,' I was told.

A heavy line is felt to pull back the rod tip on the back cast. If properly designed, a light rod performs the same way, but it is not easy to feel this. I had changed my own casting style to improve performance, giving that sought-after narrow loop. This was done by abandoning the traditional 'elbow joint' action in favour of the shoulder. It takes time and patience to overcome years of muscle-memory, but the result was remarkable. But was I going to take on the whole fly fishing establishment, as did Skues, who had scars to show for it? No. I was not. I was content with a hundred or so connoisseurs.

There was yet another fallacy I had to expose. This was the fear that such an ultra-light outfit could not play and land big fish. The answer for me and my friend, Joe, was to catch some big fish. We planned a 'Round Britain Quiz', to chuck flies into streams and lakes, coming down from Caithness, through Sutherland to the Scottish borders and on to the Welsh Marches via the Ure at Thornton Watlass, in Bedale.

Joe and I were fortunate to plan our trip in the twentieth century. Whilst I was loading the tackle into the car I smiled to myself. There came to mind a tale I discovered in the *Fishing Gazette*s of yesteryear. It was in the late eighteenth century that three London anglers planned their annual holiday in the Weald of Kent. They took a boat down the Thames, landing at Gravesend. The anglers being of moderate means, the holiday was to be on foot. They fished the Medway at Yalding, but they had to leave the village in a hurry as one of the party cast lascivious glances on a local maiden. Her swain, a robust son of the soil, took exception to this and advanced with fists flailing.

They followed the river bank to Tonbridge where they put up at a hostelry called the Black Horse. Sharing a bedroom, they were so assailed by rapacious bedbugs that they had to sleep on the floor.

Next morning they vented their spleen on the landlord who assured them: 'There is not a single bedbug in my house.'

'You are right,' one replied. 'There is not a *single* bedbug here. They are all married with large families.'

I had long been captivated with the idea of fishing in Caithness, which is as far North as you can go without falling into the sea. I had once read a story, called *A Place of Stones*, of an impoverished family who bought a cottage there, with some land from which they hoped to win the wherewithal to survive. The brave attempt lasted just a few years before the relentless landscape defeated them. So I was somewhat

150

surprised when we found that the cottage we had rented on a farm near to Wick was by fertile pastures, with handsome felt-coated cattle and plump sheep, my dear old Romneys which were indifferent to moist marshland soil.

Some of us love those moorlands which lie under spectacular skies, the cloud castles by summer's day, the Merry Dancers by wintry night. I sympathise with those Ely fenlanders of old who went from place to place on stilts, and freely gained all they needed in fish and fowl from their watery plains. Then came the Grey Men, the men with souls of lead. They drained the fens and enclosed the land. The fenlanders resisted so fiercely that they were named as 'tigers' by the Authority which hanged or transported them. Why, I wonder, do we always lose? As a politician once sagely observed: 'The power lies with the people. Thank God they don't know it!' Once in a long while, though, the towers of Bastille do come tumbling down.

So it was with the Flow Country. True, it had its share of Grey Men who covered the land with Sitka spruce. The earth could not breathe. The lochs remained with God's own trout. Here was the loch of Toftingall, beloved by the Queen Mother who had her picnic baskets packed once or twice a year so she could sally forth from her frugal Castle of Mey to watch the ospreys plunging down to seize their fish dinners. Close by was the Bloody Moss where Vikings slew Caledonians. And not far away Sir John Campbell of Glenorchy marched his hairy-kneed clansmen to collect an overdue debt from the reluctant citizens of Wick. Cannon and claymore won his day in the last great clan battle, so a memorial by the River Wick reminds passers-by.

We came there in the time of the mayfly. Before the change in the calendar long ago, when people rioted because they believed the Government had stolen eleven days from their lives, the male spinners did dance in May. Their days were stolen too, and now they arrive in June. It's curious, our

151

angling scriveners rhapsodise of the clouds of Green Drakes which bejewel the surfaces of the chalk streams and Irish loughs without realising that here, in the Far North, the lady spinner would still flutter into a huge swarm of male consorts, rising and falling between the conifers.

We preferred to fish by wading the shallow margins. It is not simply economics; ten days of boat and motor hire is not cheap. The boat angler catches more fish, with his knees cramped to below his chin, and he understands what a pain in the arse really means. I love bank fishing; it suits my casual ways, of sitting down by the reed beds with a flask, to watch the oyster catchers and divers or to find a pink orchid in the cotton grass. I know why the Queen Mum came here, and I know why the local fishermen willingly spared her a day or two of peace, as they spare Mr and Mrs Osprey a trout or three to share with their young.

The hot-spot was a peninsula on the far bank. The amiable breeze was over our shoulders. It formed an oily slick of a wind-lane within casting distance. The hatching duns seemed to stick there in the surface film. The trout knew that. And so did we. It was a heart-stopping business to see the natural fly taken, and another. My Olive Bumble patiently waited for the approaching trout, leisurely cruising upwind. Then the swirl was there, my fly was engulfed. Striking, the light rod was bent down into its fighting curve. The Toftingall fish are of the moorland colour, sepia, and splashed with scarlet as if that sanguinolent stain from the Bloody Moss had bedabbled them. Not the biggest fish in Caithness, and not as bright as the silvery Loch Levens from Watten, you still achieve your 'pound Scottish trout', and one day, dropping a Blue Zulu over a weed frond, I managed to hold a two-and-a-half-pounder out of its sanctuary … maybe it's better to be born lucky than good, eh?

We proved the ultra-light line rods in Caithness, on Watten, being squired in a boat by the genial Hugo Ross; as a fishing tackle dealer, he has his place reserved in Heaven. Then on to the home of big, but dour trout, the little loch at Sarclet from whence you can hear the angry North Sea ravening on the rocks below. Here Joe fought a lusty-two pounder which fell to his March Brown. One day we had the vast Loch of Calder to ourselves, nary another two-legged silhouette on miles and miles of bank. Calder fish are usually small, mahogany fighters, but here and there patient anglers take the monstrous Ferox cannibals which lurk in the deeps, but scour the shallows at dusk or come inshore to prey on the spawning char in early season. Calder fish hit the fly with such speed that the Southron visitor, staring at an empty whorl where his fly used to be, will plaintively ask his native companion: 'Exactly when do I strike?' 'About two seconds before you see the rise,' is the unsympathetic answer.

It's not often that an angler confesses to failure. I confess to be addicted to the Cross Lochs, in Sutherland. This is a nest of five lochs, resulting from marl workings long ago. Two of them are the homes of large fish, sought by those who have an empty glass case to fill. I was tempted by a remark made by Bruce Sandison, the patient searcher of distant lochs. In his book, *Trout Lochs of Scotland*, he told me: 'They can be the most infuriating waters in the North.' Every time I visit Caithness I take the coastal road, turning off towards Forsinard where I buy a day-permit to fish these enigmatic lochs. I drive for miles, upwards along a forest track until I reach the barrier where a hand-written card displays an arrow pointing across a wasteland of heather, bog and peat hags. It is an arduous walk, best taken with a compass bearing from the map, not forgetting to make a note of the reciprocal bearing for the homeward trek.

This last pilgrimage, with my friend Richard, was no different to the previous ones. We reach what seems to be the loneliest place on earth. A mournful wind stirs the reeds, where a bitter ripple glitters under a steely sun. This first loch is as clear as Caithness glass. There is fly; plenty of it, including those succulent marbled sedges. Yet no sign of a moving trout. I have yet to see a rise here. Perhaps the insect life is so rich on the lake-floor that the great fish have no need to break surface. Or is it as Richard says: 'There are so many huge trout here that they daren't leap out of the water for fear of there being no room for them to get back in again'?

Hour after hour we ply our lines, fishing from the surface to the bottom, without any result. I recollect Bruce's other words: 'There are times when you'd swear there wasn't a single fish in them.' My friend, Jeff Sage took a fine three-and-a-half-pounder here, on a Teal & Green (he is one of the last traditionalists). We sit on the bank where we look into the clear water only to be taunted by shoals of minnows and scuttling water-boatmen. The sun now goes to bed below the conifers; their shadows lengthen. So, hot and sweaty, and smothered in deer-ticks, we go bog-hopping from tuft to tuft until, exhausted, we reach the car. We sink a pint or two in the Forsinard Hotel and promise each other we will never return ... and yet ... and yet ... 'Did you not see that eagle over the loch? Was it a golden one? It was too dark against the sky. Or could it have been a sea-eagle from far-off Rum?' The mystery still holds us. Oh yes, we will return.

'At least we know why they're called the Cross Lochs,' I tell Richard. 'I've caught nothing and I'm bloody cross!'

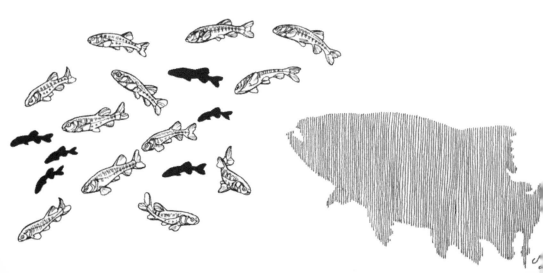

# 13

*All their life was spent not in laws, statutes or rules, but according to their own free will and pleasure. They rose out of their beds when they thought good, they did eat, drink, labour, and sleep when they had a mind to ... in all their rule ... there was this one clause to be obeyed:* DO WHAT THOU WILT

– François Rabelais, *Gargantua and Pantagruel*
*(The Abbey of Thélème)*

THOUGHTS OF A Utopian existence always come to me when I am strolling in sunlight along the banks of the Seine in Paris. It was here that I met the bearded, gigantic anarchist who offered me cheap red wine in a rusty tin mug. No vintage ever tasted better. I wonder, who were the anarchists who would have joined the Rabelaisian monks in the mythical abbey of Thélème? The valiant knights in Thélème were free to go a-hawking or a-hunting, these gallants, in the company of handsome ladies mounted on 'dainty well-paced nags'. No mention of fishing. In the real world as the next best thing to his ideal, Rabelais recommended the Abbey of Bourgueil. I would have joined Rabelais there, for not only do the vineyards of Bourgueil produce my favourite *rouge*, but the nearby Loire is well endowed with fish. Isn't that Utopian enough?

Yet here I am on the concrete quais of the Seine. And here I meet a lone roach pole addict, the inevitable black bottle and baguette by his side. Never utter those words of a Jonah to a French angler: '*Bonne chance?*' So I enquire instead: '*Ça mord?*' Yes, he has some roachlings for his evening *friture*.

And so we talk of fishy things. He waves the stem of his pipe vaguely in the direction of the Île de Cité. 'You know that's where they burned Jacques de Molay, the Grand Master of the Templars?'

I can assure him, I do know. That genius of the historical novel, Maurice Druon, recorded in *Les Rois Maudits* that Pope Clement and the King, Philip the Fair, had decided to destroy the chivalric order of Templars. There were many reasons. Those knights were blamed for the failure in the crusades. Their secret order had become enormously wealthy and powerful. They had secret ceremonies which were said to be heretical. It might have been a coincidence that the King was short of a few million francs at the time and could have used their treasure. The chief Templar was Jacques de Molay and he was in for a hot time.

The slender tip of the float is unmoving, so again his pipe points over the river. This fisherman is a history buff. 'They tortured Molay. He confessed to heresy. But then he retracted his confessions as having been made under torture. So the King erected a stake on the island and watched the execution from the window of his palace there.'

I recollected the memorial plaque in the Place du Vert Gallant. 'Ah, but as he was being burned he cried out that he was innocent, and summoned the King, the Pope and the Archbishop of Sens to join him before God's judgement seat within the next year. They all died within that time, didn't they?' I asked.

'Oh yes,' he replied. 'The King was not impressed with that summons, but confessed that he had made a mistake. Not in refusing pardon to Molay. Oh no. But in not tearing out his tongue first. And they never did find that treasure.'

They fish so fine, these anglers of the Seine. The miniscule tip of the float gives the ghost of a quiver. The angler lifts his pole, then slides in a tiny roach which could not resist the boulette of scarlet Mystic paste on his hook. This

Mystic paste is why I seek a *marchand d'articles de pêche* in Paris.

I knew its inventor, Bernard Crassat. He used to be a carpenter. One day he arrived at the lake without having brought his *asticots* (maggots). It was too late to return home. He hunted in the boot of his car. The only thing he found was a tube of reddish glue, a remnant from his trade. In forlorn hope, he squeezed some of it onto his hook. To his amazement he began to catch roach. Thus was born his little factory which produced 'Mystic, the King of Baits'. Fishing one day with my friend Henri, I rifled through his tackle bag for the bait box. 'You've forgotten the maggots!' I yelled. He laughed, and he tossed me a tiny tube. 'That's all you need,' he said. I caught roach that day on an evil-smelling red glue. My best redfin on Mystic was a fatso of 1 lb 10 oz. God knows why they take it. Would you swallow a spoonful of balsa cement? But they do.

My first expeditions to France were to catch zander. They were scarce in England until some adventurer released them into Fenland rivers. I stayed with Henri in Dieppe. We had to collect some live bait in the lakes at Arques-la-Bataille where long ago the Protestant claimant to the throne, Henri de Navarre, lowered the boom on the army of the Catholic Ligue. It was peaceful, that day we fished. The chain of lakes lay in a valley below a range of hills from which height an impressive forest frowned down on us. Henri, a zander specialist, told me that each bait-fish needed to be of exactly the right size, a few centimetres long. Trouble was that French anglers prized this size of roach for their fry-ups. The bigger roach were discarded with disgust and chub were beyond the pale. Even so, the Mystic paid off. We caught a dozen or so.

Next morning, in the darkness before dawn we set off to the zander lake. I think this was at Jumiège. At that time night fishing was forbidden, so we joined a queue of vehicles lined up before the gates at the entrance to the lakes. As dawn was breaking, the gates were opened and the 'gold-rush' began for the most popular swims. I was learning that French fishing habits were different to ours, for the live bait-fish were threaded up on traces as they were in England in the nineteenth century, before trimmers and gorge-baiting were outlawed. As each 'sandre' was floundering in the shallows. Henri rushed into the water and savagely drove a gaff into its flank. The zander is a knife-and-fork business in France; the sentiments are much the same as when a deep-sea trawler man unlooses the gasping fish from the cod-end of his net on to the deck when the trawl is brought inboard. It is a different 'philosophy' (that word again!).

Days later, strolling around the harbour at Dieppe, I explained this to a giant herring gull, perched on the prow of a fishing boat. It examined me sympathetically with its yellow eye, then dipped its beak in agreement. I did not convince a fellow countryman. I was dining with him in London. I told him how we fished in France.

'Gaffing and gorge-baiting! Ugh! Those Froggies are bloody barbaric,' he exclaimed, pausing between mouthfuls of a delicious Lobster Thermidor. I failed to tell him that his lobster had been plunged alive into boiling water by the chef just a few minutes before. 'Alas for Human Nature, especially other people's,' as a cynical French savant once remarked.

The most scrupulous fishery managers I met were in Austria. I had been invited to join my friend Manfred to fish the River Alm. The Alm is a mountain torrent, until eventually it tumbles into the Traun, that famous grayling haven beloved by Charles Ritz. Manfred was a member of the club. Although he was allowed to take me to the stream as a guest, he was allocated days to fish the Alm, just eleven times a year.

Firstly, we had to go the fishery office to obtain my permit. This stretch of the Alm was administered by a monastery. We climbed the creaking stairs and we were ushered into the presence of an elderly monk. He examined me as if he were a zealous border guard interrogating a terrorist suspect. My details were entered into a passbook, height, colour of hair and eyes and so on. He handed me the pass with a gentle smile, and off we went to the Alm.

I saw at once that it would be impossible to fish upstream, even though garbed in thermal chest-waders. The torrent thundered down and it would explode all over me if I dared confront it. The secret was to slide into the water, to face downstream, to go with the flow. Even so, it pummelled my back. I was startled to see that I was actually fishing down-hill!

Austrians prefer grayling to trout. I understood their respect for the Lady of the Stream. On being hooked she erected that striated dorsal fin, put herself sideways to the current and bent the rod into a hoop. Austrian rivers and Austrian fly fishers break all the rules; they have to. The dry fly, well-hackled in that turbulent water, is thrown down and across the current. Drag is concealed by the knotted surface of the stream. I chose unwisely a white sedge fly. Soon I lost sight of it as flurries of snow flakes whirled down even in the crystalline sunlight. It was like hiding a leaf in a forest.

I waded cautiously down the middle of the river. Manfred was leading the way, some fifty yards ahead. Suddenly he let out a yell and disappeared. He had slithered on the long chalk ledges on the floor of the stream. He emerged, shook himself, laughed and fished on. As luck would have it, we were fishing in September, just a day after the trout fishing closed, and even though the targets were grayling, I latched on to trout after trout which had to be released. Austrians are natural sportsmen who understand conservation. They are welcomed on our grouse moors, unlike shooters from other lands who blast off at flocks of starlings put up by the beaters.

As dusk fell, we took ourselves down to the small town of Kemmelbach where we hung ourselves from bars in the local swimming baths to have our aching muscles massaged by the jets of warm water. That night I was lulled to sleep by the mournful sound of the hooter on a barge as it passed my dormitory, on the bank of the Donau; a grey ghost-bark, sliding through the river mists, as the one which bore away King Arthur to Avalon, long ago. Next day Manfred saw me to the train.

'I had an idea that the Hitler family once lived in Kemmelbach?' I said. He studied me with gravity, then replied: 'But that family came originally from Bohemia, you know.' I didn't know.

'I was sitting next to that ass Anthony Crossley and when any remark was made deprecating the Germans he cheered lustily ...' so said Neville Chamberlain during the Munich crisis in 1938. You have met these two before and I was mystified as to how that doughty Edenite, Crossley, met his death. An official biography told us that 'he was killed in action off Denmark on the 15th August, 1939'. As the war had not started, this seems unlikely. I am minded to accept the unofficial account that he was hurrying back to have one last fling at the enormous sea trout in his beloved River Em as he knew he would be embroiled in the coming conflict. I believe his aircraft crashed and he was killed.

This Swedish river is a legend. It belonged to a family of aristocrats, the Ulfsparre, so in those days fishing was selective. The Count had his circle of friends. Even so, famous fly fishers of the day managed to fish this river which is short in length before it is swallowed up in unfishable marshland. The size of the fish is due to their larder in the Baltic where they gorge on strøming, similar to sprats. The best and most hazardous fishing was by night. Two famous pools on the Em are named after worthy angling writers of that time. They are the Barrett and Lawson pools. Barrett invented a capital fly for the Em sea trout, a confection called 'Moonlight on Mrs Higgingbottom', which I wrote about in *To Meet the First March Brown*.

Alas, I was somewhat short on influence and blue blood, so I never fished the Em. Whilst manning a stand at a Game Fair in Sweden, though, I was close to the reputable House of Hardy where the genial Jim Hardy was showing his firm's classical rods to the local anglers. One day I noticed that he was missing, so I asked his stand-in where he had gone.

'Oh, he's off for the day to fish the Em,' he told me.

On my return to my own booth I noticed that the walls of the tent were lit up by a green light, shining from my eyes.

The magic of Sweden did not relax its grip on me, and I coaxed an invitation from the famous lady fly-dresser Margrethe Thomson to fish her stretch of the River Atrann. Then one night I joined a party of fishermen to fish a lake deep in one of those troll-ridden dense pine forests. We arrived at the lakeside on one of those calm evenings when the surface of the water is an unmoving steely sheen. We caught nothing. Seemingly a party on the opposite bank were denied sport, for a fire flamed beneath the pines and the waly-waly of a tragic song floated across the lake.

'It's a regular party from the Soviet embassy,' explained my friend. 'Obviously, they've caught nothing. They've hit the vodka and now they're feeling very sad.'

'Russians are a very sad people,' I replied.

'Tonight they've got a lot to be sad about,' Gøran said.

Then there came from the depths of the forest the cry of a soul in torment. 'What's that?' I asked fearfully.

'Oh, it's a bird, only a loon,' Gøran explained.

'Loon?' I enquired. 'From what family?'

'The Loon family, of course.' And all the Swedes fell about. That is what passes for Swedish humour.

I was staying in a cottage on the crest of a hill overlooking the village. The sombre pines marched right up to the garden fence. In the morning, awoken by a scrunching sound, I saw from the window that the head of a giant elk protruded from the trees and it was scrumping the crab-apples in the garden. I also noticed that some two dozen elderly folk were sitting in the garden, enjoying the view over the small lake.

'Anyone can go anywhere in Sweden,' Margarethe explained. 'Those are people from the old folks' home.'

So, I travelled on to Finland.

'We're going to fish for perch.' I was invited.

'Where?'

'Down there.' My guide pointed to the Gulf of Finland.

'But that's the sea! Salt water!'

He shrugged. 'Oh, the fish are used to it.'

And so they were. It was weird. We went afloat. Great steamers passed us by whilst we twitched the spiny zebra-fish out of the ocean.

Next morning early I strolled in the park in Helsinki. A young girl came up to me, speaking in an incomprehensible tongue.

'Sorry, I'm English,' I told her.

'Oh, English. Give me money,' she demanded.

'No!' I said, and received such a powerful kick on my ankle I thought it was broken, as she ran off.

At ten in the morning drunken couples were swigging vodka on the park benches. So, when I was invited to take a sauna, I declined.

'It's good for your health,' they expostulated.

'How come that Finland has such a high rate of heart disease?' I wanted to know.

'We throw red wine and vodka onto the hot stones, then breathe in the fumes,' they explained.

162

So I watched the little red locomotive pass the window of my hotel, on its way to Leningrad.

I had been invited to participate in a Game Fair in Denmark. I found it impossible to avoid taking part in a casting tournament. Although, like most anglers, I get a little smug satisfaction when I catch more fish than my companions, competitive fishing does not appeal to me.

Once I found myself on the banks of Lough Conn. My friend, Mike Tolan, was organising the famous Wet-fly contest and some ninety hopefuls had arrived from all corners of the globe to take part. I declined to fish that day and took myself off to rest my back against the walls of the lakeside monastery where, in days gone by, unfortunate travellers seeking a night's hospitality were blinded by having a red-hot iron seared across their eyeballs before being turned loose on the highway. This day it was peaceful. It was like the W. B. Yeats' famous 'Innisfree' hearing 'lake water lapping with low sounds by the shore'. I sighed with contentment, stretched my legs out under the sun when Mike arrived to spoil my day.

'My boat party has not arrived. Can you make up the number?'

He had prevailed on Dr Whitaker to join, the famous state banker whose name appeared on all the Irish 'Punt' banknotes. I was persuaded, for the good doctor's delectable home-cured ham was even more renowned than his political reputation, and I could share it on the island at lunchtime.

We were both at a disadvantage, for Mike had not told us that our boat would be the last to go afloat as he had to shepherd all the other competitors out on to the Lough before the starting gun. I confessed that I had no competition experience at all; this was to be my first and last trial, and that as a personal favour to Mike. Yet it was a glorious day with enough lops on the waves to help the struggling Green Drakes to clear the sticky surface film.

The strange thing is that I won. This was due to two things. I did not fish the usual team of four flies on a short line. I tied on two flies because I am the world's greatest tangler, especially under the eyes of others, and I feared to disgrace myself by fumbling with 'birds' nests' when everyone else was happily fishing. I tied a Silver Invicta on the point and a large Olive Bumble on the dropper to simulate the mayfly duns. My first advantage was due to my modest physique. When I fish the usual loch-style, dibbling flies close to the boat, after a while my right arm wants to drop off to find relief from the dull ache. So, unlike every other fisher that day, I threw a long line and retrieved the flies 'on the pull'. Perhaps the water was too clear for the short line, but that was how the trout wanted to see the fly.

The second advantage I had was a hat festooned in flies. Two trout were hooked at the same time. Panic! They dived under the boat, and as I spun round the line became entangled in these flies. I dropped the rod and played the fish from my headgear, so that Mike was able to entrap them in his boat-net. Even so, with only four fish and a tummy replete with the best home-cured ham I had tasted, I weighed in four fish, that being the winning score.

It had been a Brahma of a day. At midday the boats went ashore for lunch. There's obviously some Gallic blood in the ancestry of the Irish race. Some anglers had time to nip down to the bar in Ballina to refill flasks ... alas, not all competitions are so relaxed.

Driving back to the ferry port I saw passers-by waving and laughing as I passed. I wondered if my fly fishing fame had spread, until, stopping for petrol, I discovered that some wag had written with his finger on the dusty side-panel of my car the legend: 'Brits Out!'

English anglers are besotted with the Emerald Isle, myself

no exception. A friend, having repaired to a lock-keeper's cottage by the River Barrow, invited me to fish for the legendary bream. They are superhuman monsters which place their enormous girth and slab-sides across the fierce current to put an intolerable strain on nerves and gear. The secret is to bait up the night before with a sackful of mashed potato and rusk. The hot spot was to fish from the grave-yard of the local church. All went well; I caught some respectable Irish bream after first having won a stout contest with a sunken supermarket trolley.

The congregation eventually left the church after morning mass. Then the young priest emerged from the porch, fag stuck on lower lip, cassock hitched up to allow him to thrust his hands into his pockets. On seeing me, he sauntered across to ask the inevitable question: 'Any luck?' To which I answered with my customary modesty.

On remarking on my accent, he put the question: 'Are you by any chance an English Catholic?' I thought to myself that I must box clever.

'Oh no, I'm an agnostic.' That will fool him, I thought.

He removed the cigarette from his lips, studied the end of it thoughtfully, and then continued: 'But are you a Catholic agnostic or a Protestant agnostic? We only have the two sorts in Ireland.'

Then, chortling to himself, he wended his way to Murphy's Bar in the village street, reminding me never again to get into theological disputes with the Irish; you can't win. They are too subtle.

But here I was in Denmark filled with trepidation, for how was I going to look respectable in the casting tournament when faced with these giant young Vikings? Again, Providence came to my aid. Space on the ground was limited, so the event was to be for accuracy, to throw the flies into a series of hoops. I was the only one who had served an apprenticeship on the River from Hell, the Kentish Teise.

Having won my sole fly fishing match thanks to a fortuitous hat, now I managed to hit the targets from kneeling positions, from under branches, into the wind. I did win, and I quit whilst ahead, making a resolution never again to be seduced on to the tournament platform.

I had been invited to Denmark by the fabulous fly-dressing expert known as 'Steff'. He took me to the River Simisted to fish the floating fly on the evening rise. I felt at home there. It was a slightly milky chalk stream with native brown trout eager for the fly. Just as I was lining up a regular rise my eye caught the portly figure of someone crossing the cornfield towards us, imperturbably brushing aside the waving crop like a galleon in full sail, breasting the ocean's crest.

'Why, that's Preben,' said Steff. His voice quavered a little, his hands trembled. I did not realise that Preben Torp Jacobsen was second only to God amongst Danish anglers. We were invited back to his house to be regaled with that fiery Schnapps which paradoxically comes so cold from the freezer that it rims the glass with ice.

Preben could claim to be the last traditionalist. He formed the split-cane for his own fly rods and even found a way to compress the linseed oil onto tapered silk to copy the fly lines of the Golden Age. He was a vet, and a recognised expert on poultry; I could imagine him chasing a terrified cockerel around the barnyard to snatch a shiny, bright hackle feather for his Iron Blue Dun.

I was so mesmerised by Preben's expertise that I realised that I would need two lifetimes to master the art of fly fishing. I explained this to my parish priest when I returned to England. I asked him if he would put in a request to the appropriate Authority, to which he must have had a priority connection. Like young Oliver, I wanted a second helping.

He smiled sadly. 'No, you must be satisfied with the

three-score-and-ten, or thereabouts. There can be no exceptions.'

'What about Methuselah?' I wanted to know.

'Don't believe everything you read,' he advised me.

# 14

*If I had been born an idiot and unfit to carry a gun –
although with plenty of cash – they would have called me
a Grand Sportsman. Being born poor, I am called a
Poacher.*

*A Victorian Poacher: James Hawker's Journal*

THE BOOK FROM which I have quoted is a fascinating
insight into the mind of a poacher who was driven to
poaching by poverty and a harsh life. This is a far cry from
the modern poachers who are simply criminals out for gain.
On occasion Hawker had to steal hares or starve. And he
also kept the wolves away from the doors of other poor folk.
He was one of those extraordinary countrymen who, though
quite unlettered, had a way with words. A spark of genius
perhaps lay in his subconscious, but as with the rural poet,
John Clare, the urge to write was irrepressible. The flames
burst forth and decades later, a retired surveyor, Tudor
Walters, invited his friend Garth Christian to visit him to
inspect his collection of birds' eggs. During this visit Garth
Christian noticed a bound volume in the library of the
house. On opening it he discovered the hand-written
memoirs of the Victorian poacher. The Oxford University
Press is to be congratulated on publishing one of the most
remarkable social histories of our epoch. Read this captivating book for yourselves, for it was published in 1961, and it
became a paperback in 1978. You will rise at 'peep of dawn'
with James Hawker and watch him slide his little rifle from
a special pocket fashioned in his trousers. Then, with his
deadly aim, he will pick off a hare.

You will understand, too, the hard times which he endured in the village of Oadby. This gave him a lifelong Socialist faith, and he justified to himself this way of shortening the gulf between his life and that of the landlords who preserved the game for the affluent and privileged. I make this point only to draw a distinction between those criminal townie poachers of today and those countrymen poachers of yesteryear who were driven by hardship.

Hawker is not my preoccupation. Indeed, he seems to have neglected fish; the only ones he mentioned were pike which rarely he sought with gorge-baited line and trimmer. His main quarry was the hare.

In a fishing life, especially if you are after salmon, it is likely you will encounter the traces of the professional poacher. It is weird that anglers recognise and respect the social divide between coarse fishermen and trout anglers even though today's living standards have eroded much of the difference of the twenties and thirties. I believe there is an even wider gulf between the fly fishers for trout and those who pursue salmon. It is not simply that salmon fishing is more expensive. There are many 'open' beats on famous salmon rivers where a day or week permit may be purchased at reasonable cost. The trouble is that the urban salmon fly fisher has to book his holiday in advance, only to be told on arrival at the fishing hotel: 'There's been no rain for weeks. There are no fish in the river. You should have been here last month, we had a bonanza then.' The privileged man receives a message in his office: 'The fish are up.' He books his helicopter and within hours his ghillie hands him his rod and stands by with the net and Nitrolingual pump spray.

Even so, this fisherman is not depriving the local poor; there are none. He may excite some envy, and this may explain, though not excuse, the poacher who creeps to the river by night to empty a tin of Cymag into the pool. This is a highly toxic cyanide compound used in horticulture, etc. He scoops out his poisoned fish but also kills every living thing downstream, perhaps for miles. The poison deprives the gills of oxygen but does not contaminate the flesh, so the fish are sold, no questions asked. Whereas a Victorian poacher would go out alone or with one companion, today poachers go out mob-handed. Apprehended, they use violence whereas Hawker would simply outrun the game-keepers. He kept himself fit.

My first encounter with the poaching gang was on the River Ilen near Skibbereen. I was night fishing for sea trout. Arriving at dusk, with no one in sight, I waited patiently until those seven stars glimmered above. As I slipped into the water I realised that there was such a cold wind that I would need to fish upstream. This brought me down to a single, black-hackled fly which I threw upstream onto the surface of the pool. My nerves were jangled when a weed-bed at my feet suddenly heaved itself upwards. Then the head of an otter emerged, grinning at me. A herd of white horses thundered up and down the bank behind me. Amazingly, I had one of my best catches within two hours, some seventeen peal and an estuarine slob-trout. It was glorious fishing, each fish coming to the surface to take the fly so that I could see the swirl in a glint of reflected light.

Keeping an eye on the frisky horses, I was walking back along the bank to the ford when I saw the glow of a cigarette. Coming nearer, I met two groups of men, one on each side of the river with a net across. My first thought; how lucky I was to have taken my best catch above them. I had to reach the ford below, so I passed them nervously, calling out 'Good night.' 'Good night, sorr,' was the cheerful response. On reaching the home of my friend, Arthur, a water-watcher who was putting me up, I told him of the incident. Hardly taking his eyes off the TV, nor putting down his glass, he said, 'Oh yes, it's those lads from Cork again, I suppose.'

There is still the occasional enterprising loner. I met one by daylight. I was bream fishing on the River Barrow. I walked by a relief channel, past a sluice. To my astonishment there was a man standing on the apron of the weir with a garden fork in his hand. He had turned down the force of the water to a shallow stream. The foolish salmon were still leaping onto the apron and floundering in the thin flow. He pitchforked them onto the bank. He gave me a friendly greeting and asked me if he could give me a fish or two. I declined, pointing out that the fish were red. 'That's their spawning stage,' I told him. 'Oh, I won't be worrying about no spawning stages,' he laughed. I could see that there was already a sizeable heap of gasping salmon flapping on the bank.

I seemed destined to bump into poachers when I went salmon fishing. This was a challenge to my conscience, because part of my escapism must be due to a lack of moral fibre. I could not bring myself to 'grass them up' to Authority. It was also clear to me that local people were aware of what was happening; they probably had salmon steaks in their freezers. Cynicism salved my conscience.

Many years ago I had booked a week's salmon fishing from a hotel by the Tweed. On the first evening, joining a party of regulars in the bar, I was introduced to the 'Walkerburn Angel' which was widely used up and down the river.

The trick was to fasten a huge swivel to the tip of your fast-sinking line. Then you added a yard or two of lead-cored line, plus a short, but very strong nylon leader. The 'fly' was a heavy metal tube with just a few wisps of feather to make it legal and a great treble hook protruding from its rump. A skilled practitioner – and over many years he had plenty of practice – could feel his line go across the back of a salmon. A powerful snatch would drive the hook home in its flank. This was the ignoble art of 'sneggling'.

I declined to use this device. I often wondered afterwards, was it due to an unaccustomed surge of moral courage, or did I admit that I lacked the necessary skill to use it? Who knows?

That same week my innocence was again put to the test. It rained. I decided to go down to the river at first light as the salmon would 'be up', and the other guests still abed. I had noticed a shed in the garden, so I stored my rod there, overnight, already made up for the fray. As I walked along the path before sun-up I heard heavy footsteps pounding along behind me. As I opened the shed door a hand fell on my shoulder. The landlord and I stood amazed at the sight of two large gunny-sacks, opened at the top to reveal that they were filled with gaffed salmon.

He looked at me, seemingly bereft of words. Then he stammered, 'What did the bloody fool leave them here for?' He paused, and then continued, 'I don't know what this is all about, Geoff, but I'll find out and speak to you later. Anyway, there'll be four fish in the boot of your car when you leave.' Funny thing, I don't much care for salmon!

In the evening he came up to me. 'This is what happened. The local poacher had gaffed the salmon on the beam weir, but he was chased by the police as he came off the river, so he ducked in here and hid the fish in my shed without telling me.'

Later, it all ended in tears, some of chagrin, some of hilarity. Authority outlawed the celestial tube fly. It blew up the beam weir and the local poacher sold his gear and wore mourning black for a fortnight. He had been a celebrity and on a previous fruitful occasion he sold a couple of dozen salmon to a rich, though incompetent, angler staying at the hotel. This worthy had his photograph published in the angling press. He stood proudly, dressed in full fig and with rod in hand; the fish were tastefully laid out before him, spoils of the chase ... but some of us noticed the autumnal leaves scattered thoughtfully over the salmon, just where you might expect to find the holes made by the strokes of a gaff ... if you had a suspicious mind, that is.

This happened so long ago. I was a young novice with the two-hander at the time, and Tweed was my jinx river for salmon; I lost the fish I hooked. There was a happy incident to balance the ledger. A companion was fishing with me on Juniper Bank. We were chatting to a novice opposite who was making a pig's breakfast of his line management. He was frustrated. My friend had just landed a five-pound sea-trout which the other man had not noticed. We suggested he was using the wrong fly. If he cast it over to us we would change it for a certain killer. The fly landed near to us; we switched it to a better pattern, then firmly hooked the still-lively sea trout to it, without him seeing this. We pushed the fish and fly back into the water, telling him to recover his line. After a few feet he felt the fish kick. 'Well done!' we yelled. 'You've done it, you've got one on.' He reeled in the freshly run fish, bright as a silver florin. We shared his delight, and he never knew what we had done.

There is a legend; I believe it rings true. There was a respected salmon fly fisher who ran fly fishing courses in our riverside hotel. This time he had a party of beginners to instruct. The Monday, all went well. In the evening he told this flock that he and a colleague had been invited to fish next day on one of the most prestigious beats on the river, an opportunity for which millionaires shelled out thousands of pounds. He could not afford to pass it up. For that one day the pupils would have to fend for themselves.

That day was all tribulation for them. It was a time of tangles, of wayward casts, of freezing water overlapping waders, even tumbles into unknown holes – and no fish. Tired, angry, cold and wet they straggled back into the hotel. There, in the hallway were the silver salvers for the fish they had not caught. Instead there were five splendid double-figure salmon, each bearing the name of their instructor. In the bar he regaled them with his exploits, salt in their wounds. After the evening meal it was noticed that one of the fish had gone walkabouts. The Great Man was not amused.

'A joke's a joke,' he told them. 'I can take a joke as well as anyone. That's an end to it, though. I'm going to have a bath, after which I expect the fish to have been replaced.' It wasn't. 'It's just plain theft,' he exploded.

Then it turned sour. He was incandescent with rage. He prevailed on the landlord to search the guests' rooms, with no result. The atmosphere in the bar was poisonous, so the Great Man took himself off to his room for an early night. Resplendent in his silk pyjamas, he pulled back the bed coverings to see a beautiful salar laid out on his bed sheet. I doubt he saw the joke.


My friend, Colin North and I had booked a week's salmon fishing on a good Scottish river, which will remain nameless. The cottage came with a long pool of high renown. The most prolific pool was below us, but the proprietors, having a fishery business, only netted that pool earlier in the season. We had booked ours after the netting had finished. Consequently we paid a higher rate. And we knew another angler had taken the fishing below.

We fished hard that week. We neither saw a salmon, nor turned one over. Yet the river seemed to be in good order after recent rain. One day, in frustration, we strolled down to the pool below, hoping to exchange gossip with the other rod. To our consternation we saw a netting party at work. Angrily we accosted one of the men. 'Oh, the angler cancelled his booking and as the company couldn't get another rod at such short notice, they decided to net the pool this week to recover their losses.'

In a high temper we drove down to the town. We demanded to see the Director. He stayed hidden, refusing to see us.

Whilst we were consoling our spirits with different spirits

in the local pub another angler added to our woes. He told us that the Saturday night before our arrival, the Dumfries gang, whose poaching notoriety was bruited abroad, came to net the pool below. They made a magnificent haul. As dawn was breaking, in their hurry to leave the water their van collided with a car, killing a young mother and her child. Dozens of salmon were scattered over the roadway for the police to find.

Colin and I sought restitution in law and we did eventually recover our money from the proprietor. Later, I was told that those fishing rights were acquired by the Atlantic Salmon Trust, so the legal netting was ended ... but the illegal? Who can tell?

I am uneasy with salmon fishing traditions. The social stratification which has largely died out between coarse and trout fishing lingers on in salmon fishing. Symptomatic of this is the ghillie who must always call you 'Sir' (or 'Madam' should you be one of those bold female adventurers who challenge our sexist sport). At lunchtime the ghillie will creep away from the fishing party to quaff his single malt and munch his game pie in splendid isolation.

Such a ghillie was bestowed on me on the banks of the Braes beat on the Lower Spey. He was a dear old soul, one of the old school.

'What's your name?' I asked.

'Gordon,' he replied. I was perplexed.

'Is that your surname?'

It was. So I said, 'Look, stop calling me "Sir". I have not been knighted and never will be. What's your Christian name?'

He was embarrassed. I pressed him.

'It's Woollie,' he replied eventually. 'Woollie' is Scots for 'Willie'.

'I'll call you Willie, and you'll call me Geoff. OK?'

'Yes, Sir.'

I gave up.

There is also a tremendous jealousy in salmon fishing, especially when it comes to fishing rights. On being invited to fish a beat on the Royal Dee, I was cautioned not to wade further than halfway across the river. Eagle eyes were watching from the far bank, so much so that at dusk, fishing for sea trout, I was blinded by a flashbulb exploding on the far bank. I was being photographed by the water-watcher. He was familiarly called 'Haemorrhoid Henry'. The law, it seems, is different in Scotland. You may wade halfway across the river to fish your fly down the far side. Their anglers' Devon minnows will strike the water by your feet. I had the last laugh on this stretch of the Dee, for the owner placed white paving stones as markers in mid-stream. Happily they were a yard further over than my usual stopping place. I hooked a grilse under his feet. I could not have reached it before.

Legal actions over boundaries are like Jarndyce and Jarndyce. They keep barristers in bread and honey for generations. Yet the river changes. The winter floods come, shifting pebble banks from place to place, and last year's salmon lies have moved ... what do the lawyers make of that, I wonder? You may believe that life is too short ... you would be right, for it is not unknown for death-bed promises to be given for the next generation to pursue the family feud down the years. Until, perhaps, global warming will inundate low-lying land to end for ever the runs of migratory fish.

Even the poacher of old didn't have the last laugh. Many a river has its 'dead man's pool'. Sometimes it's where a sudden bore-wave catches an angler unawares. He fails to hear the menacing roar of the approaching surge which overwhelms him. The Findhorn has such a bore-wave. Sometimes, though, a poacher ducks under the surface to elude the water-watcher, and he drowns, to give lasting fame to the name of the pool. Was this not true of the Torridge? My friend Richard, perhaps he put it all into perspective. We were roach fishing on the Medway when I caught a wristy eel.

'D'ye know, the flesh of that thing costs more than fresh salmon, pound for pound?' So I sent it back on its journey to the Sargasso Sea.

# 15

*He strode off with a fisherman's ponderous gait,*
*All out of granite crudely hewn, strode as men stride*
*through gunfire,*
*through the ages . . .*
*. . . He resembled Hemingway so much! Later I learned*
*It was indeed Hemingway.*
Yevgeny Yevtushenko, 'A Meeting in Copenhagen'

To CONSIDER HEMINGWAY is to hold a candle to the sun. You see, this page might well have been a blank. Halfway through this book I have run into a writer's block, a disease familiar to all wielders of the pen. The virgin screen stares back at me like a relentless Cyclops. This syndrome has its casualty lists. Poor Hemingway believed his talent had deserted him, so sucking the end of a shotgun he blew out his brains. Nearer to home, a lesser known novelist, but one of great craftsmanship and a personal acquaintance, Frank Tilsley also believed that he had written himself into the ground, and fell on his own sword, so to speak. It is serious, you see. I believed that Frank was at the height of his powers. He was one of those working-class writers who adopted a folksy style which was popular, so much so that his book *Mutiny* became a much-praised film called *Damn the Defiant*. The dreaded block blots out all self-esteem under a black cloud of depression.

I thought of a remedy. For some years I was the editor of a modest newsletter for a game fishing association in Kent. It was impossible to persuade the members to write contributions. It was like taking Rip van Winkle in his early morning cup of tea. I bethought me of a friend of many summers who agreed to help me on two conditions. The first was an amiable idea that we should meet in one of the pubs in the Weald where they sold Biddenden cider. We would converse on current fishery topics. The second condition was that his purple prose would appear below his chosen pen-name of 'Jack-by-the-Hedge'. Now Jack was also a homespun amateur shrink on whom folk with personal problems could rely for common-sense advice. I carried the pages I had written to the restored priory where he lived.

'I have a problem,' I told him. 'I've run into a writer's block.'

'That's not a problem,' he answered. 'That's a disease!'

Later, we sat side by side to be mesmerised by the scarlet tips of our porcupine floats as we tempted roach in his nearby pond with multi-coloured maggots writhing in a heap of sweaty sawdust at our feet. 'Your problem is you decided to walk down a sunny memory lane. There are shadows in real life which you disregarded. But you admit to being an escapist. Your readers will want to know what you were escaping from. Now, I reckon that if you make a habit of suppressing the bad memories you'll wind up with so many neuroses that you will have to consult a therapist. Tell me, did you ever consult one?'

'Oh yes, my wife persuaded me to visit one when I was depressed after my fishing tackle shop closed. I met her about four times in a narrow, bare room with my couch on one side and her chair opposite. She clutched a black book. I thought it might be the *Book of Common Prayer*.'

'And what did she say to you?'

'I can only recall two phrases after I had told her my complete life story. The first was "I think you've had a traumatic life". "The second?" "Are you going to pay me now?" She once accused me of trying to entertain her, but I was only attempting to fill the vacuum with one-sided conversation. So I also lent her a copy of *Fishing Days*. After four sessions she told me she could not see me any more.'

Jack was silent for a few minutes, digesting this information. Then he asked: 'Did you ever find consolation in religion? I know you love old churches.'

'I had regular home visits from two sweet, elderly ladies from the Jehovah Witnesses. I asked them in for a cup of tea and we discussed the Origin of the Universe. They were very strong on theology but rather weak on particle physics so we did not get far.'

'How long have I known you?' he asked. 'Must be about fifty years or more? We met again at a dirt track motorbike race meeting at Wormshill. Let me throw a shadow or two into your book. You once told me of a school friend you fished with when you were in that boarding school. The headmaster was what we now call a paedophile. How did you escape from that?'

'We were not like the kids of today, street-wise. The most our parents told us was not to accept sweets from strangers. Tony and I discovered a small pond just outside the school limits and we sneaked out to fish for crucian carp. I remember that day when the sky was filled with planes towing gliders to the Battle of Arnheim. That was the day they found Tony's body. He was lying face down in the grass, apparently suffocated. By then everyone, boys, teachers, parents knew the man had killed Tony. He escaped justice because the Home Office pathologist messed up the post-mortem. They brought in a verdict of misadventure. But the school closed and I went home.'

'Did you ever meet that man again?'

'No. In 1968 I was recovering from viral pneumonia. I was confined to bed for several days. My temperature leaped about like a deranged skylark, but in the boredom of lucidity I read the *Guardian* from cover to cover. There was his unusual name, A. G. P. Austin. Identical to the Austin I knew, this man also preferred to use his third Christian name of Philip. When I knew him he was some 31 years old. This 'second' middle-aged sexual predator was 54. Everything pointed to the two Austins being the same man. I recollected that his family home was in Liverpool with his mother. He had been arrested and interrogated about binding and strangling a young man after a sexual assault. At a police press conference it was revealed that Austin had five previous convictions for sexual crimes, in three of which he used drugs.

Whilst in custody he committed suicide by swallowing sodium cyanide. The subject Austin taught at my school was chemistry.

I should have followed it up on my recovery. I did not do so. In my muzzy condition I had not made a note of the police station in question. I made myself a vague promise that I would investigate it some time when business pressure was less competitive. And perhaps I was wary of becoming ruled by obsession. The friendships we make at school are amongst the strongest relationships we make in our lives.

You see, Jack, you *have* awakened my conscience. I promise you that I will try to track down this homicidal paedophile.[1] If I succeed, I promise you that the story will be written in a second edition of this biography. And if I succeed I can challenge the 'misadventure' verdict of the inquest on Tony's death. I promise to do so.'

I reflected on this conversation. There is no reason why an autobiography should not be selective, simply because our own memories are selective when we dip into our subconscious minds to entertain ourselves. When I am in the bath in a somnolent state I conjure up visions of the Old Weald when I was a boy. Of course there was harsh reality, the neglected farms with their unkempt hedges, the heaps of unharvested apples rotting under their trees, the piles of furniture on the cart in front of the tied cottage from which

---

[1] See the end of this book in which I tell you how I kept this promise.

181

the labourer and his wife and children were being evicted because he joined a Union.

Today the farms are prosperous. Labourers are few, the Luddites have gone, replaced by machines, and the worker is as much technician as tiller of soil. Out of the distant haze comes the roar of traffic on the motorways and overhead a plane takes holidaymakers to places unknown to the labourers of yesteryear; there is no escape from the Grey Men with their souls of lead, save for odd stretches of the Teise where the church bells of Horsmonden and Goudhurst talk to each other across the valley as they did in days of yore. And commuters strolling past the church at Goudhurst are blithely unaware of the niches in the graveyard wall where yeoman of old sharpened their arrow-points when practising for the fields of Crécy, Poitiers and Agincourt.

There am I as a boy, trotting caterways through orchards or hop gardens to fish secret ponds untouched by fishing rods since the Huguenots dug them centuries ago. In those days farmers had too many worries to chase small boys who went fishing, save one we called 'Buller', he of the chimney-pot hat, the shaking stick, the raucous voice and scarlet cheeks. This farm was wonderfully named as 'Old Hay' which explains why Buller was anxious to keep boys out of his meadow grass. The amber chub-stream sulked under the sun in high summer whilst the sleepy chub, almost too lazy to move, would occasionally sample a delectable insect trapped in the sticky film of the water.

The trick was to tie a length of flax water-cord to the tip of a tapered garden cane. Two mayflies would be impaled on the hook, fastened there by a yellow wild flower, say a buttercup. The cheven would saunter up to the temptation, fall for it and then hell would be let loose. Without reel or net we had to turn the bolting fish from its holt, then drag it up into the meadow grass. As luck would have it, that would be the exact moment when Buller would forge through the sea of grass, smoking with fury like a battleship at Jutland. We had to grab fish and tackle and outrun him to the gap in the hedge.

Chub, when cooked, have been described by trout lovers as a mixture of needles and cotton wool, but our villagers loved to eat them. Often I wondered if it would be a good idea to bake them according to Izaak Walton's mouth-watering recipé which involved sewing up the chavender with a pound of butter in its cleaned-out belly, not to mention many herbs.

'It's better to eat the plate and throw away the bloody fish!' I was cautioned by a knowledgeable chef. Nor did I ever upset fanatical carp anglers by cooking their quarry, though on one occasion at an exhibition in Paris I was offered a chunk of baked carp-meat on a stick, a present from the genial chef of the 'Tour d'Argent' of gastronomic fame. I understood why the Poles and Prussians preferred it to the tasteless turkey savoured by heavy smokers with their deadened taste buds in English suburbia at Christmas time. So I asked my friendly French chef if he ever cooked chub. He looked surprised, smiled sardonically and shook his head.

# 16

*Lo, the unbounded sea . . .*
Walt Whitman, 'The Ship Starting'

'I'LL SETTLE FOR one dark shadow,' said Jack. 'But I notice you like to poke fun at yourself. You put yourself down. Now, you have your own blank pages to fill, a fishing life of five or more decades. You must have caught some notable fish, so what about some boasting? Another angling writer would revel in that opportunity. For example, what were your biggest fish?'

'Jack, you won't believe it, but I've caught more big cod than any other species . . .'

I can tell you a true story of the discovery of *every* angler's dream, a miracle bait. I was laid up with a tummy bug so I had to give up my place to catch cod in the club's boat outing. A couple of days before the trip the club Chairman rang me up.

'We got a replacement for your boat place, Geoff. Sorry you can't make it. You know the club rule. Booking fees are not returnable. The skipper says that conditions at sea should be perfect.'

'That's great, Ken. Where are you heading?'

'He's taking us to the Heaps Bank as they are catching heaps of cod there. Get the pun, Geoff? Heaps and heaps?'

'Sorry, Ken, I'm fresh out of humour today. All set then?'
There was a slight pause.

'One niggle, Geoff. You know it's been difficult getting bait. I've arranged to collect lug and rag worms at the harbour tackle shop, but the dealer warned me that *live* bait is getting hard to find. So fingers are crossed.'

'Ken, I might be able to help you. You know I am writing an anthology of old fishing magazines?[1] I came across this tale from 1879. A boat party made a huge cod-killing using strips of raw tripe for hook-bait. The cod couldn't resist it.'

'Tripe? Well, they take squid, don't they? How did they use it?'

'They cut it up into long strips which they hooked at one end. It wiggles about in the tide, smells good and tastes just fine. As you know, cod are the billy goats of the sea. They eat anything.'

'Thanks for the tip, Geoff. I'll get some from the butcher. It will be a safety-net standby.'

'It seemed to be a miracle bait for the Victorians. Ring me after you get back. And save me a plump codling.'

Ken rang me.

'How did you get on?'

'Geoff, it was a disaster! The tackle dealer had no live bait for us. He sold us some stale squid and some dried-up black bootlaces of lugworm, well past its shelf-life date. We fished hard all day. No one had a single bite. We gave the tripe strips a good swim! Starfish adored it. Cod ignored it. For twenty quid a head we caught bugger-all. There's a club meeting next week. I have to give them an explanation about your miracle bait. What can I say? Why did it fail?'

'Maybe the skipper anchored the boat in the wrong place?'

'No way. The licensed victuallers were some yards up-tide of us. They were hauling in heaps of cod from the Heaps Bank. Any other daft ideas, Geoff?'

'You didn't cook it, did you? I said to use it raw.'

'Of course we didn't cook it. I bought some extra for our table. It was all together in the fridge.'

---

[1] *The Bright Stream of Memory* (Swanhill, 1997).

'Oh, of course! Tripe goes with onions. Cod hate onions. Did you put the tripe into a dish with onions?'

'Not on your Nelly. I add the onions whilst cooking for the table. I kept the bait separate. Come on, Geoff. You've got to help me out. They'll have my guts for garters unless I can give them a reasonable explanation. Why did the cod refuse to swallow our tripe?'

'All I can think of, Ken, it may have been something to do with the date?'

'The date? The date? . . . What's April the . . .' Ken broke off; he seemed to be choking . . . then he roared down the phone, 'Oh, you cynical bastard!'


I have always loved the sea. As a boy I heard it in its anger, thundering against the old sea wall at Dymchurch. When the fishing tackle trade unexpectedly gave me a few years of affluence I decided to buy a small fishing boat. She was called *Audrey* and I moored her at Bradwell-on-Sea. I knew nothing of boat handling, nor of navigation, so I put myself in the hands of a fierce red-haired ex-Navy instructor on the Solent. He explained how to fix a position, to calculate a course and read a compass.

I was bewildered, crouching at a desk in the cabin with the problem he had set me. My first fix seemed to sail our boat through the fair fields of Hampshire, attempting to justify King Charles' ship tax to John Hampden's puritan landlub-bers. That caused civil war, but my martinet teacher looked over my shoulder and said succinctly: 'Bollocks! Start again.'

Eventually, slinging my kit bag on my back I left the estuary with a certificate to say that I had passed tests in boat handling and navigation, so now I could use my ship's radio and buy diesel fuel out of bond.

*Audrey* was a chugger. With friends, I was able to coast along the Maplins at about four knots. This was to spot the gulls swooping along a reef where bass were driving the baitfish shoals against the sky. The sea boiled; the bass were having a ball.

Let me explain. My interpretation of Bernard Venables' 'happy to fish for anything anywhere' persuaded me to skip from one species to the next. Some double-figure pike, my appetite was jaded . . . move on to carp . . . but they were not the intellectual elite of fish; after all, the boilie-boys had cracked that. I had my share of 'doubles'. There remained the mysterious sea and of all its inhabitants the handsome, athletic bass mesmerised me.

Bass loved those shallows along the Maplins and sand flats. It was a lonely place. The army had built gaunt towers on the Red Sands and the Shivering Sands. There they mounted their anti-aircraft guns. Long since deserted, the wind moaned through the rusty girders, the laments of the souls of drowned sailors in torment, for many a raider sneaked in to drop mines in the Thames approaches. Where the tide hits one of their victims the sea is churned into a maelstrom. This was where the giant bass lay in ambush amidst the wrack-covered spars. It was patient fishing, to winkle a rag-worm through the snags of Davy Jones' locker. This is where I caught the ten-pounders. The big bass are solitary stalkers.

School bass hunted in packs. The brit would be harried along reefs. Once we found their killing grounds it was our turn to murder, to spin a sand-eel through the pack. The trick was to avoid the commercial boats which kept a watchful eye on anglers. When we saw their heading come round to our quarter we knew they had found our shoals on their sonars. We wound in our lines and setting the motor at full speed we ploughed up the bass shoals and scattered them to the four oceans.

Years later I allowed myself a secret smile to see the bill of fare of a restaurant in Greenwich announcing 'bass baked in Pernod' as its speciality. In those early days we could not give bass away. Fishmongers optimistically labelled them as 'salmon-bass' to tempt the cod-eating monomaniacs in London. The commercial fishermen sold their catches to France. Even taste buds have their fashions.

Bass were the fish of summer. Winter swept the Essex marshes like the Angel of Death; the Siberian wind. The cod rejoiced, they followed the arctic wind and water. They hugged the bottom as they moved inshore to harvest those giant king ragworms, the piercing jaws of which made me wince when they caught my fingers as I threaded them up the hook-shank. The Essex anglers had discovered a revolutionary way of fishing these shallow seas where the tides raced. Gone was that short, powerful traditional boat rod which plonked a pound or two of lead onto the sea floor. A graceful, light ten-footer replaced it with a small multiplying reel of freshwater size. The lead weight was a mere few ounces though with wire spikes which would spin open to release the weight under rod or fish pressure. The baited line would be cast up-tide. The tide would lock the weight into the sea-bed and the rod tip would bend into a graceful arc. When a fish took the bait, hooking itself, the rod would straighten, and the captive fish would drift weightlessly down-tide towards the boat. I could never tell whether I had latched onto a small whiting or a coal-scuttle mouthed twenty-pounder. It was when I applied the pressure to lift a big fish from the sea floor that all hell would break loose. The rod would buckle, the tip plunging into the surface, and sweat would start from my skin as I pumped the brute towards the hateful light. It was a deadly method. Glancing through my scrap-book I noticed a photo where a grinning *Cygnus* party stood behind a pile of forty roker taken on two tides and over seventy big cod were boated on another day. Our best bass catch was eighty-eight fish, but all save four fish per angler were returned.

Unlike other fishing, except for my addictive roach, I never tired of up-tide work. My mistake was my own human nature.

I longed for an even bigger, faster boat to prospect further. It was a time of my affluence, the late seventies, the last boom-time for the fishing tackle trade before leisure habits changed and recession came. I went to Plymouth to be seduced by *Cygnus M*. She was a chubby lady built on a broad-beamed hull. We fell in love and we eloped back to the Essex marshes.

I have to admit that I was addicted to Admiralty Charts, a hangover from my Solent days. I had long been fascinated by the Galloper Bank which lay athwart the tide races some forty miles to the east of our berth. Up to that time, as far as I knew, and the lightship crew confirmed it, no one had fished the bank. The ground was too rough for expensive drift-nets or trawls and the distance too far for inshore angling boats. I knew it would be easy to find if we set off at dawn to home in on the light-beacon. Friends did not take much persuading, so loading fresh vegetables, milk and newspapers for the light-ship we set off on what must have been an anglers' 'first'.

It took four hours to reach the lightship. We were welcomed with mugs of 'marine' tea (you can stand a spoon upright in the stuff) and we feathered up mackerel bait from the stern before setting off along that narrow strand which would be a few feet under the surface at high tide and a cricket pitch at low water, if you had a mind for it. We hit it at the ebb and a squadron of screeching gannets were plunging in to show that there was a feeding frenzy in play. One of our party sent down a flight of feathers, staggered to see a frayed length of his line blowing away in the breeze. The Galloper mackerel were the largest I have ever seen.

I had baited a mackerel and dropped it on a heavy weight to the sea floor, but the line went on paying out, yard after yard.

'I can't hit bottom,' I yelled. As I started to rewind, the line surged away from me and I brought a fine tope to the surface. A shoal of tope had joined the feast and before any bait could hit bottom it would be wrenched away. It was a day of magic which comes once in a lifetime; we boated fourteen different species of fish. The westering sun told us that it was time to point the bow into its crimson mouth, to head for home with cheery waves from the lightship men, who soon were to lose their way of life as their lightship has since been replaced by a Lanby buoy. 'Everything has its vermin,' as Blake sagely remarked. Yes, the Grey Men even rule the sea with their account books.

There is a price to pay for flying too close to the sun. My Icarus was the larger boat which, to help mooring expenses, I foolishly let out on charter. I found it with the engine seized, the deck burnt away and a complete rebuild necessary. One gleam of silver in that dark cloud was that I indulged myself with a powerful new diesel, a new teak deck and redesign of the interior, raising its speed from eleven knots to over twenty. The Essex marshes lost their charm, scene of one painful memory, so we left by early light, arriving on the Sussex coast in the dark to follow the 'leading lights' to new anchorage.

Recession came. *Cygnus M*, arguably one of the best angling boats around our coast, had to be fed into that melting pot, by auction emerging into another Universe in Belgium. Her short reign in my heart caused a strange reaction in my head. After her I was never able to set foot in someone else's boat. I know the ways of commercial skippers. When the tide is running at the end of the day, as the fish are starting to come, it's 'Wind up, lads, tea-time, that's all for today.' Or, should I join a party in search of turbot, a lonely quarry which has to be hunted with care? After an hour or two the impatient skipper will cry out: 'That's enough of that, we'll move off the bank into deeper water for round fish.' It's selfish and egotistical, I admit, but after *Audrey* and *Cygnus* I could not be in a boat where I was not master, fishing the way I wanted to fish in the places of my own choice. For specimen hunting at sea you need to be master of your own destiny.

That's how it was in tropical waters when Bernard Venables quested for his mighty six-gilled shark. That's how it must be when you drift a live launce along the sloping edge of a sandbank, down-tide in search of the turbot . . . but other anglers will tempt you to move to the shoals of easy fish. This was the choice off the Essex marshes. The mark known as the Maplin Spit was the winter home of big cod. They were few and far between, a long cruise towards the booming guns of the Naval testing range. The commercial angling-boat skipper has to satisfy his paying customers. I did not. And I was infected with the specimen hunting bug.

Yet in that short time we missed several rod records by ounces, including the crab-crunching smooth-hound, a pound and a half short, and a cod of over thirty-one pounds. We might have had the red gurnard record but a knife-and-fork man claimed it for his pot. Our best bass weighed fourteen pounds. It all had to end. There was a home-grown recession in Westminster and the toll on fish began to punish stocks so much that we witnessed the sad plight of proud men scraping a living by trawling for seaweed for Christmas decorations.

Thereafter I was on the lonely beach of Dungeness by night, watching the satellites wobble overhead and listening to the roar of sea on shingle, the sound which Matthew Arnold heard so long ago on Dover beach, 'where ignorant armies clash by night'.

I received a call from my friend Oscar. He runs a bakery in Switzerland, so he never fished in the sea. He was coming on holiday to England. Could I spare a day to take him beach fishing? Could I not? I had come to love beach fishing. Yes, I could. The pain of losing my beloved boat was being ground away from my heart.

I longed to return to a magical place of my boyhood at Folkestone Warren. Memory produced a romantic image.

The beachcombers were dashing into the tidal flow to scoop up whiting in buckets. But that was long ago. And they do warn sentimentalists: 'never go back!'

There were high chalk cliffs behind a belt of woodland. From there a path descended to the beach. The beach was strewn with rocks and pools. Arriving at low tide, we used to mark patches of charcoal-grey sand between the rocks. These were targets for our bait when the tide filled. To cast into the rocks meant losing tackle.

After our long journey to the coast a sad sight met my eyes. My romantic beach had vanished, a casualty of climate change. Our chalk cliffs rest on bases of softer rock. The beach of memory was now under an apron of concrete, though this was a firm base for our beach-rod tripods.

Oscar caught two shining bass. Bass ride the second roller of an incoming tide. They pry into rock crevices for food. I glanced up at the towering chalk cliffs behind us. As school-boys before the War we were marshalled on the Lea to join the crowds witnessing the passage of the giant German airship, the magnificent Hindenberg, scouting along our Eastern coastline on its trial flight. The airship's military passengers photographed our airfields and coastal defences.

We had a glorious day of bass fishing.

I thought about the exhausting trudge back to the car park. My subconscious mind kicked in another memory. 'Oscar, I know a short-cut back. See that building on the cliff top? That's a tea room. There's a zig-zag path up the cliff-face. Another woodland path leads to it. It's a steep haul, but it will save us an hour.'

I found the first path. We trudged uphill as it wended its way towards the base of the cliff. Disaster! Our pathway was blocked by an enormous rock-fall. My obliging memory revived the great storm of a fortnight before. Happily, I could see the zig-zag path beyond this heap of rocks. Bootmarks on the chalk showed that walkers had scrambled safely across.

As we hopped over the rocks, another unexpected sight met our eyes. There were bouquets of fresh flowers with an occasional wreath. On to the tea room, and sinking in front of steaming mugs, we asked the waitress about the floral tributes. 'It's been in all the papers,' she said. I told her that we had come a long way and we were unfamiliar with her local media.

'Tell us what happened,' I implored.

'It was the night of the big storm. Fierce gales. Torrents of rain. You saw that house on the cliff road? Man, wife and two daughters? Husband hated cats. The family doted on a Siamese, called Hecta. He planned to get rid of it. The night of that storm was right for it to disappear with no blame to him. When his family was in the Land of Nod, wrapping the cat in sacking, he sneaked out to the edge of the cliff. He was about to chuck it over the cliff when the ground gave way beneath his feet. He is buried under such an avalanche of stone that they can't recover his body. They held a service down there and we left flowers and wreaths.'

'What happened to the cat?'

'Oh, she jumped clear and made her way home where she now lives in peace. She was soaked to the skin when she arrived. Happily, one of the daughters owns an electric hair dryer.'

My friend Joe Tingle boated one of those giant skate when fishing off the Irish coast. It weighed over one hundred pounds. He described the fight as trying to stop a runaway billiard table.

My ambition was to catch a giant halibut. I went to Orkney. I met one of those unusual boatmen who promised to stay at sea overnight if necessary. Jimmy took me out with two Danish anglers. We boated shedfuls of haddock, cod and ling. The water was clear, the colour of aquamarine. It was my delight to lean over the gunwale to watch the occasional cuckoo wrasse being brought to the surface. It shone like a fluorescent Pirandello when hit by the sun's rays. I am told that although eating wrasse is like munching pin cushions, they do make a delicious soup.

Although we fished around the Old Man of Hoy and further afield, the legendary monsters of Orkney failed to favour us. I took myself off to Denmark where I shared the amazing catch of garfish with the local tackle dealer. We were casting spinners from the strand. The garfish were so numerous and eager that they fought each other to grab the lure, even trying to tear it from the mouth of another hooked fish. They chased the lures almost to our feet. We crammed garfish into our waders. Invited back to supper, my friends turned off the light so that I could see the skeletons of these garfish glowing luminously blue in the dark.

Then I crossed to Sweden to spend a week at sea with my friend Olof who edited a fishing magazine and also owned a sumptuous fishing boat. We were going to sea in quest of the rare Greenland shark. There was a spare bunk for me. I booked my flight to Gothenberg.

Memories crowd in. The Swedish entry for the Americas Cup was being put through its paces off Marstrand. Its crew was paranoid. Any craft approaching within a half-a-mile was driven off. Even so, *Svengsta* did not win the trophy that year. Whilst Olof was hanging over the stern to gaff a cod for me he cried out that a great halibut had followed my catch up from the bottom, only for it to dive down again as it grew frightened by the sunlight. That was the nearest I got to a giant halibut.

It is a strange thing that when coarse fishermen were besotted with specimen hunting, I became disenchanted with it. Yet as it was almost unknown by sea anglers, big marine specimens were my target. When my boat *Cygnus M* was rebuilt to my own specifications, a speed of up to 22 knots permitted me to fish up to fifty miles from the coast. At Brighton Marina we heard rumours that porbeagle and blue shark were being seen at some distance from the coast. I reasoned that if we could locate shoals of pouting, which were plentiful, the chance was that shark would attack them. I had fitted a superb fish finder which could scan the ocean many metres around the boat. We located the pouting.

I had attached a live-bait rig to a metal line of some 40 lb breaking strain. I lip-hooked a live fish and dropped it to the sea-floor. After some time a furious downward movement of the rod-tip showed that the bait had been taken. On striking, I realised that I had hooked an immense predator. My friends gathered round whilst I started to horse it towards the surface, all the time checking its sideways lunges. The trick was to hoist the fish upwards for a yard or so at a time, with a rest in between hauls, then reel in line fast as the rod was lowered. I think I had the monster half-way up when it must have seen the glitter of sunlight above.

It made an unstoppable dive for the bottom. The steel line twanged and broke like cotton. We had no idea what fish had taken the bait. Opinions varied from a giant conger to a big porbeagle shark. The bait-fish was a pouting of about a pound and a half. It was taken in one gulp. I was shaking like a leaf in a gale, and saturated in sweat. It was the heaviest fish I had ever fought. One companion remarked that whatever it was, if it had climbed into the boat he would have jumped overboard. 'There's not enough space in your cockpit for me and a pissed-off porbeagle,' he declared.

I am still haunted by dreams of the Blackwater estuary. There is nowhere like it in this world. I see it when the wind drops at sunset and the western sky is aflame. *Cygnus* is drifting quietly home across the sands. A roker (the local name for a thornback ray) lazily flaps its wings in the calm surface. A stately Thames barge is hunting for a slight breeze in the channel. Far off is a friendly landmark, the oldest Saxon chapel of this land, reclaimed from its use as a barn.

The earliest Christian communities were here, until the year AD 991. '*And in that year it was determined that tribute should be paid to the* Danish *men because of the great terror they were causing along th*e *coast ...*' (from the Anglo-Saxon Chronicle).

Should I tell you of the 'Song of the Battle of Maldon'? The Vikings landed on an island in the Blackwater. The thegn raised the local fyrd to form the shield-wall to deny access to the invaders from crossing the narrow causeway to the land. The Vikings claimed this to be unsporting, so the Men of Essex graciously allowed them to cross for a fair fight. Bad move. As the Americans say: 'Never give a sucker an even break.' It was their own shield-wall which was broken and the Viking 'Land-waster' banner of the black raven floated victoriously over the Saxon dead. Yet there must have been a Saxon war correspondent who fled the field of blood to a distant monk's cell to write the first epic poem in the English language. So, sit by the ancient churches on the far shore, a day when all is at peace. Take a few pulls on your hip flask of Rémy Martin. Then lie back in the long grass. The estuary will be spread out below you. Half-close your eyes. You will see the far-off points of light gleaming on swords and spears; you will hear the clash of steel on steel, the war-cries of warriors, the groans of dying men.

Time can run backwards, you see. It does in this book.

# 17

*They fuck you up, your mum and dad,*
*They may not mean to, but they do.*
*They fill you with the faults they had*
*And add some extra, just for you.*
                                                    Philip Larkin

WHEN I WROTE *Fishing Days* back in the sixties I wouldn't have got away with the 'eff word' but now it's common currency in the media, though this time it's the poet Larkin whose immortal words are on the desk of every psychotherapist in this land. Oedipus, eat your heart out! It is unfair if personal experience is any guide, for the implication is that incompatible parents who detest each other should stay together for the benefit of their children. Alas, no matter how careful they may be to keep their feuding private, 'not in front of the children', inevitably the tensions leak out at the breakfast table. The children understand plain honesty in relationships. So, when I declare that were it not for fishing the graveyard or the madhouse would have claimed me long since, I must confess that being brought up in a dysfunctional family forced me to seek an escape route with a roach rod under my arm. I must explain without throwing too many shadows over the sunlit water.

Visualise the small Wealden hamlet in those fraught years leading up to the last war. My father was the village schoolmaster in a Church of England school. In those days of moral hypocrisy, unless the rupture in the familial relationship was hidden from the local gossips both he and my mother, who taught in that school, would have lost their

197

jobs. Nor was divorce easy; today the courts throw it at you. Their only route would have been to collude with a seemingly adulterous partner, paid for by the night. The private detective would burst into the bedroom in the early hours with the flashbulb of his camera exploding over the 'guilty' couple in bed. It's weird, over fifty years later, talking to old inhabitants of the village; no one knew that my mother and father went their separate ways at weekends with their chosen partners whilst I was farmed out.

Sometimes I was with my school friend's huge family in their tied cottage, crammed into a damp bed with two other boys and a heated brick wrapped in flannel. This cottage had a dark pond at the bottom of the garden which we had stocked with roach taken from other places. On occasion though, I was lodged with a widow, the school cleaner, a Mrs Cook. I had to cross the forstal in front of her house to find another pond, rush-lined, beneath the inevitable Bramley trees. Here I fished alone; here I learned how to enjoy loneliness. The roach were of good size as the only other fishy inhabitant was Nature's pruning hook, the pike. It was exciting to shin along a branch overhanging the water to glimpse the 'Luce' sunning itself in the shallows whilst unconcerned roach fussed about in front of its eyes until some mysterious change took place. Maybe the predator's dorsal fin quivered in expectation of its dash into the shoals. The would-be victims scattered in panic. The pike is not the superb killing machine described by some naturalists. It is inefficient. I have watched it for hours, launching itself futilely at its dinner table, but some instinct warns the prey a split second before impact; the shoal scatters. The pike misses its target, spins round on itself in frustration. Were this not part of Nature's checks and balances these orchard ponds would soon be bereft of roach, to be dominated by the starving pike of legend until it wasted away. Nature has built into predators two safety mechanisms: inefficiency in stalking and sheer indolence. A famous pike-watcher once told me that one of his targets went on a feeding spree about once every ten days.

It's not entirely true that after my very short political career I never again joined a political party. Later in life I was tempted by a group of environmentalists who sketched out an intelligible conservation programme on the back of an envelope whilst quaffing a few gills of nectar in a pub. This was the Ecology Party. It did not last long before being swallowed up by the Green Party, like a small roach which blunders into the maw of a 'pike in the reeds'. I was not comfortable in the Green Party. I crossed swords with those members who hankered after an imaginary chocolate-box dream of a rural community living on a vegetarian diet from the meagre earnings of cottage crafts. Nor did I relish their antagonism to field sports which they failed to understand. For were it not for hunting, our landscape would have ceded the patchwork quilt of hedgerow and hanger to borderless plains of jaundiced rape. But for anglers taking polluters before the magistrates our rivers would have become polluted sewers bereft of wild life.

I did enjoy one séance with the ecologists before they surrendered to their Big Brother. We sat cross-legged on cushions to delve into the memories of the lives of our forefathers. We all lived and worked in an urban environment, but almost without exception, our grandparents and great grandparents were country folk who lived in the fens or the broad acres before migrating into the city slums and 'satanic mills' after the industrial revolution. They took with them their rural sports and thus there was the burgeoning of the Victorian fishing clubs with the cheap rail fares provided by the dear old *Fishing Gazette* of yesteryear. They were more than fishing clubs. I was invited to speak to one of the oldest, the United Brothers of Deptford. Their meeting room was in a pub not far from that famous creek where

Nelson's 'first rate' ships of the line would have been immortalised on the canvases of local daubers. As I gave my talk the beady eyes of stuffed fish-trophies glared down at me from the bow-fronted glass cases where they swam unmoving between fronds of reed and rush which never grew.

On leaving the pub late that night, waiting for the bus in Deptford, I met the modern example of urban man in the shape of an Irish drunkard who asked me for a fag. 'Sorry, mate, I don't smoke,' I told him. He staggered towards me, saying, 'You fucking Limey,' and swung an inaccurate haymaker which missed its target, my head. The momentum collapsed him in a heap onto the pavement where he remained stupefied ... I apologise for the political incorrectness and the obscene language, but am I to exclude political incorrectness in favour of basic Anglo-Saxon we all use in private, and the thought that Irish are no more drunkards than the rest of us? I could as easily encounter a souped-up Englishman. No, plain honesty has priority. It happened as I told you. And, if it's any consolation, I smile at the memory, even having sympathy for how he felt, far from the Lough and the 'nine bean rows'. I could have told him that I saw tiny flounders in Deptford Creek and once gazed in astonishment as a soaring buzzard in transit to distant moorland looked down in disdain at my upturned face, one of thousands in the concrete jungle below ... but I suppose my friend could not smell the new-harvested hay nor see Orion's Belt in the light-polluted sky ... No, he was a frustrated poet. No wonder he drank; so would I. No wonder the Deptford Brothers escaped to the river bank of a Sunday.

The Brothers were more than a club. They were a benevolent society which provided largesse for the widows and children of anglers who had joined the Great Majority. The Deptford anglers had invented the rudiments of the Welfare

State long before we thought of it. There was indeed a 'brotherhood of the angle'. It's a paradox, isn't it, that fishing flourished as the largest participant sport, nourished by hardship? There flourished the clubs and the mighty federations. Post-war, the austerity years, the Brothers would share their packets of crisps with their fellow-anglers on the way to the fens in the club 'charrer'. Then came afflu- ence with wives and kids demanding that the family car and its driver should take them of a Sunday to where the fish would be crystallised with salt and saturated in vinegar in a fish and chip bar in front of the ocean. The club's 'charrer' would be quietly rusting away in the scrap-metal dealer's yard.

It's a paradox for me, too. I was the painter's 'lone figure in a landscape', not the sociable fellow in the 'charrer'. Yet I recognise that those hard times forged that fraternal community. The escape to relative affluence destroyed the angling community and if angling is declining as I write with those clubs in the ossuary of history, then it has become a victim of consumerism where each man is an island and not part of the whole. The sad Trades Union official plaintively asked: 'How can I say to a working man with two cars and a holiday home in Majorca, "Let me take you out of your misery, brother"?'

How confused is my mind? As a compassionate man I should welcome that. And yet I hanker after that time of brotherhood, when anglers crowded onto river banks, fishing for the traditional copper-kettle prize. Why do I long for a lost world I would have hated to join? I know not, save that although they were hard times, in a bizarre sense, they had their good ways, too. What does my detachment from the present day cost me? A depth-bound feeling of guilt.

The curse of political correctness had to enter the angling world as it had in society, with the proviso that Margaret Thatcher was wrong to say that society doesn't exist. She should have said, 'community no longer exists'. There is a difference.

Even in an oblique way the fishing creeps into the labyrinthine ways of life. A friend told me of the fine catch of roach he had made in the tidal Thames near Wandsworth. At that time I was making a poor fist of line management with a twenty-foot roach pole. Remembering that the roach pole was first introduced on the Thames by soldiers returning from Picardy in the First World War, I had made the pilgrimage to Sowerbutts shop in Commercial Road in the East End to collect one of their famed miracles of bamboo, brass and crimson-thread whippings.

I had not taken into account the fierce tide-race. All day I laboured, with the line ripping the float off downstream, then hanging limply like a wet lettuce in the slack water before it decided it would be a change to nip up to Teddington. Exhausted and thirsty I set off to walk to the nearest bus stop when I spotted the bright lights of a pub. I did not know that this was the haunt of the gay community; nor was I familiar with their vocabulary. So when a young man came up to me in the bar with a friendly smile to enquire, 'Exactly when did you come out?' I replied, 'Oh, about half-past six this morning.'

Nor was I more successful with straight sex. I was late back from Tring reservoirs where I had wrestled with some slab-sided bream which generously smothered my old fishing coat in their milky slime. Anglers will know that this stuff, whilst smelling of roses in the nostrils of coarse fishermen, causes the olfactory organs of non-anglers to wrinkle in disgust. Thus bedewed with slime, plus a generous helping of squamous mud on trousers and boots, I was clattering down a side street from Piccadilly in a muck-sweat to catch the Milk Train home when a lady of the night emerged from a doorway with the time-honoured offer: 'Want to have a nice time, dearie?' She then took a closer look – and a sniff

– and pulling away from my bundle of rods and the large wickerwork basket I sported in those days, she muttered, 'Oh Christ, Billingsgate!'

You cannot be led into temptation, nor into a lady's boudoir, when wearing a fishing coat purloined from Wurzel Gummidge in a ten-acre field with a benison of bream slime and your Gorblimey trousers coated with plummy-black lake ooze. So it was 'cheerio my deario'. Now, had I gone in for a life of politics, ah, what larks, then?

# 18

*Peace, his triumph will be sung*
*By some yet unmoulded tongue*
*Far on in summers that we shall not see …*
Alfred, Lord Tennyson,
'Ode on the Death of the Duke of Wellington'

YOU MAY FIND it hard to relate these lines to the life of a
fisherman. They appeared in the letter pages of a fishing
magazine with an appeal to readers to discover their origin. I
did not recognise them even though I doubt I could live
without poetry. I wrote to the enquirer to apologise and later
received a note in which he discovered to me the author.

Yet the words are appropriate, because our Life was
described by a skald in the days of the sea-roving Vikings. It
was his task to compose a poem and recite it to the berserk-
ers on the night before battle. He told them that the Life of
Man is like the bird which flies out of the darkness into the
light of the mead hall where the heroes are roistering, and
then it disappears into the night through another window
… such is the brief time given to us in this world. And it is
a world now threatened as in the time of Noah by the rising
oceans as ice-caps dissolve in the fumes from our cars and
planes. So there will be summers which our children's children may never see. If one day the sea reclaims the Romney
Marsh to lap against the foot of the Downs, then those dykes
and canals where I floated biscuit for roach, they will
dissolve into yesterday's ten thousand summers.

I believe that like King David, setting forth to meet
Goliath, I too have descended into the Valley of the Philis-
tine, metaphorically speaking. Rooting about in the attic I

found a tattered fishing bag. Shaking it open there tumbled out a heap of obsolete tackle, cast-carriers with decayed gut-leaders and hooked flies. There was a Hardy fly reel, too stiff to turn on its corroded spindle. The silk line had oozed its linseed oil to harden around it like glue. I remember it, the line I stretched along a fence at dawn by the bank of the reservoir. This was the ritual of line-stretching and greasing, performed in haste whilst keeping an eye on the surface of the lake as the lifting mist revealed the gentle rings as trout sipped down the tiny midges for breakfast. There fell from the bag the classic 'slim volume' of poems. The pages were stuck together with mildew and fish slime, and a few fish scales had stuck to the covers.

How guilty we feel when we neglect an old friend, only to meet him again in later life! A memory came back with startling clarity. I had been stumbling upstream, a clammy summer's day on the Teise. As I reached the small bridge at Goudhurst I had had enough. I clambered up the steep bank to lie down in a streamside copse. I opened the bottle and book; the two things go together, but the murmuring stream, the soporific sickly-sweet smell of wild garlic and the warmth of the sun, they were telling me, as they told Keats long ago, that 'mortality lay heavily on me like unwilling sleep'. Was this when the fish-scales stuck to the covers? I had laid the trout on dock leaves to admire their colour. Teise trout were small and wild in those days. They took their tobacco colour from the iron ore in the clay. The bright-scarlet spots were the tears of lamentation shed for the dominance that God gave to Man over all living things, a consolation prize for Original Sin.

These were the first trout I had taken on fly. I fished alone for fear of my ineptitude being witnessed. As I lay in that spinney I saw two anglers walking along the bank, their spinning lures tinkling against the butts of their rods. I sighed the deep sigh of contentment and lay back in the tall grass to gaze at the sky through the leaves.

Gone are the days when culture-hungry Victorians ripped the hot pages straight from the presses as a great poet had produced an epic. These are the days when we confess shamefacedly to reading or writing verse, for the image of the poet is a wimp with undisciplined, curly locks, velveteen jacket, a floppy bow-tie and eyes which stare right past you into the distance ... this is not the world of a Sassoon stumbling through an enemy trench, grenade in hand, or a Wilfred Owen swept away in a hail of bullets in no man's land. And did not Homer learn his craft amidst the shrieks of dying men when Hector leapt amongst them, javelin in hand and nightfall on his face?

The time I was disenchanted with poetry was when I was scrambling mentally through the bound copies of the *Fishing Gazette*s. The first page I turned was dated 1879. I closed the last volume for 1937. I perused every page of more than a half-century. For nearly all of that time the editor was R. B. Marston who came across as a man of high integrity. He was utterly fearless in exposing frauds like George Kelson. He reminded me of that famous High Court Judge of yesteryear, Mr Justice Bucknill. He was duty bound to look over his left shoulder and sentence a ruthless murderer to death. The man in the dock swore by 'the Great Architect of the Universe' that he was innocent, which conveyed the message that both he and his judge were masons. It did not wash and he was invited to keep his appointment with Jack Ketch. So, whilst they were personal friends – it may have cost Marston sleepless nights – he did not hesitate to question the claims of Kelson who had hijacked other anglers' fly patterns and inventions and allocated them to himself, his father and companions. Nor did the great Alfred Jardine remain unscathed for claiming a false weight of a huge pike he caught at Amersham.

Marston had a weakness for bad jokes and appalling doggerel which he inflicted on his readers. I winced on reading some of the poetical efforts of his contributors.

There was one, written in Scottish dialect by R. C. B., who I took to be that redoubtable angler, R. C. Bridgett. It told of a poor wife whose husband spent all of his free time in casting a fly for trout. I reproduced the poem in its entirety in my anthology of the magazine, *The Bright Stream of Memory* (Swanhill, 1997). The woman suffered as a fishing widow. She was startled one night when her good man, who had been dreaming, sat bolt upright in bed, eyes popping out of his head, and yelled out: 'I have one on!' The wise woman found the remedy. She decided to take up the trout rod herself.

A poet can be any man or woman touched by the hand of God, even a farm labourer like John Clare. He told his townie readers how village men trapped a badger, then set dogs on it for sport. The poem was harsh and brutal. Sentimental town-dwellers were looking for rustic versifiers to give them a romantic vision of rural life as seen through syrup-coated spectacles. Not for Clare; his poetry was truth; thus Old Brock *'kicked by boys and men ... leaves his hold and cackles, groans and dies ...'* Even an angler can be a poet, a Blunden seeing red and raw Nature when the pike stalks its prey. And why shouldn't another angler carry verses in the tackle bag for those times when the dog days kill off the hatches of duns or the porcupine quill is a rigid sentinel in the heat haze over the pond?

# 19

*If any man removes a cup from another where men are drinking, without provocation, he shall, according to ancient law pay a shilling to him who owns the house and six shillings to him whose cup was removed and twelve shillings to the king.*

The Laws of Hlothhere and Eadric, Kings of Kent
(673–685)

THE SAXON WELDISHMEN must have been a quarrelsome lot. Yes, there is a fishing connection; be patient. Hlothhere was King of Kent from AD 673 to 685, but for part of that time he shared the throne with his nephew, Eadric. These laws they promulgated were additions to the codes laid down in the reign of an earlier sovereign, Ethelbert. The penalty for stealing a drinking companion's cup was severe, but as we know from the treasure at Sutton Hoo a real Saxon toper would bring his cup with him to the mead hall, a personal trophy which might well be wrought in massy gold.

We don't know much about Hlothhere other than that he seems to have been a generous ruler and a firm law enforcer. Unhappily he upset the West Saxons, who invaded his territory. He fell in battle in the year AD 685. My interest lay in my preparation of a story for the newsletter of the Kent branch of the Salmon & Trout Association. I was researching the fisheries in the Weald in ancient time. Ploughing through old records of laws and charters, the first mention I discovered was a charter drawn up by King Hlothhere in the year AD 679 in which he gave a parcel of land to Abbot Brihtwold. The book *English Historical Documents*

(Eyre & Spottiswoode, 1955) records this gift. King Hloth-here was a Christian, hence his words:

*In the name of our Saviour, Jesus Christ, I, Hlothhere, king of the people of Kent, grant for the relief of my soul land in Thanet which is called Westan ac[1] to you, Briht-wold, and to your monastery, with everything belonging to it; fields, pastures, marshes, small woods, fens, fish-eries ... Done in the City of Reculver in the month of May in the seventh indiction*

This is the earliest charter of which the manuscript has been preserved. There are formidable penalties for anyone who contravened the terms of the charter.

*They will be cut off from all Christendom and debarred for ever from the body and blood of our Lord Jesus Christ.*

Unhappily we do not know how this fishery was exploited, though the probability was that nets in some form were staked out. Both nets and fishing line were made from 'nettle-hemp'. The nettles would be harvested in spring and the square stems soaked in water for hours. After pulping, long and thin fibres would be separated and spun in a similar fashion to wool. It is strange that they do not appear to have used horsehair or even flax for fishing lines. Weights were made by boring a hole through a pebble of suitable size and shape. A hook-link taken off the line as a snood was the very first paternoster. An efficient, if crude spade-end hook of the tenth century was discovered at West Hythe, in Kent, and can be seen in the British Museum. If all this seems primitive, I remind you that my tackle as a village boy before the last war was not far removed. I was taught how to tie a flax line to an ash plant by school friends whose fathers

---

[1] This means 'west of the river'.

had taught them, as had their fathers in their time, going right back to when Hengist and Horsa leaped out of their boats near Pevensey Bay.

Although there is no record of a fishing rod being used before the thirteenth century, I am certain that the idea of tying the line to a pole would not have escaped the Saxons; the Dark Ages were not that dark!

Eels seem to have been the target. A clue comes in the Doomsday Book. There was a bounty paid on eels. The snoopers were sent by the Conqueror to every corner of England to record for tax purposes the ownership of land and property. Fisheries were included and Bilsington, on the Romney Marsh, had two, probably on the river which no longer exists, the Limen. The drains and ditches on the Marsh are famed for eels. Nearby, Appledore had six fisheries listed. The inspectors followed the Medway to Yalding (Hallinges) where they entered the facts that '*Ethelred held it from King Edward. It answered for two sulung.*'[2] They listed '*Yalding land for 16 ploughs, two churches, 2 mills and four fisheries for 1,700 eels*'. It is not until the Doomsday Book is compiled that we find regular, if sporadic, mention of fisheries and the first fish-processing plant in York.

It is strange that the Anglo-Saxons were not experienced fishermen. St Wilfred found that the folk of Sussex were starving. He saved their lives by teaching them how to fish. This is commemorated in a stained-glass window in Ripon Cathedral to which he was appointed as Bishop. And Bede tells us that this was not an isolated event because Bishop Winfred of Colchester in AD 730 '*found so much misery from hunger he taught people to get food by fishing. For although there was plenty of fish in the seas and rivers the people had no idea of fishing and caught only eels.*'

---

[2] 'Sulung' was a measure of land only used in Kent as distinct from the usual hides.

Why were eels so important to landowners? For I find no mention of other coarse fish in these ancient charters. They live a long time out of water, which was important in days when spices were costly. They are preserved by smoking without losing flavour. They are easy to catch in net and trap. It was recorded that an eel 5 feet 9 inches long, weighing 40 lb with a girth of 18 inches, was caught at Yalding in 1757. They had strong 'rough' cider in those days!

Thanet was once a real island, separated from the land of Kent by a wide river, the Wantsum. The Wantsum is a shadow of its former self. It was once a broad channel along which invaders sailed. It was a safe anchorage. On the crest of the hill above the river they built their settlements. It was the most important site in Europe to commemorate the so-called 'Dark Ages'. There were three-quarters of a mile of habitation, firstly of the Bronze Age, then the Romans built houses on those foundations and lastly came the Vikings.

I was fishing for bream in the river. Arriving at first light I failed to notice anything untoward along the Thanet Way. Leaving the stream in the afternoon I was startled to see lines of cars and coaches along the far side of the road. There were heaps of stones over which people were crawling like ants. There were cement mixers, bulldozers and earth-moving machines. I parked my car and crossed over. I accosted a young man who had collected some tools from his own car.

'What's going on?' I asked.

'They're widening the road. The old settlements will be cleared away and the site covered in concrete. I'm with the Archaeological Trust. We've been given a few weeks to get what we can and the public are allowed to rummage the spoil heaps for artefacts. It's a tragedy.'

The Grey Men had caught up with me once again.

I love Thanet; it reeks of history. Here Hengist and Horsa

landed. Here St Augustine put foot on British soil. Here, too, the Romans built their fort at Richborough. The Reculver shore was a night-fishing beach for surf-casters. The secret was to prise open a few mussels from the beds nearby to garner bait. I used to catch the right tide by moonlight when the rod-tip gleamed against the sky. It was hard to resist the soporific rhythm of the waves on the shingle. I missed many a twitch of the rod tip, sometimes finding a self-hooked codling or whiting floundering in the surf when I reeled in to re-bait the line.

Strangely, the beach never fished well by day. At noon, with a storm-tide running, the collectors would scour the shingle with metal detectors. Half a mile straight out to sea is the graveyard of a Roman port. When the inshore wind is strong, with the spring tide running with it, shards of pottery and coins are spewed up on the beach. And if Houseman's Roman soldier and his troubles are buried under Uricon, then surely the bones of Roman sailors are bleached under the spin-drift, off the Saxon shore.

This beach was nearly the graveyard of other hopes, for here Barnes Wallis tested his famous 'bouncing bomb', which later breached the dams of reservoirs in the Ruhr. With trousers rolled up to his knees he fumbled in the water for the debris of his first casings which broke up when they hit the sea.

I, too, failed. My quest was for an ancient site known for centuries by local people as 'Thunner's Leap'.

The legend has it that St Aebbe's cousin, Egbert, became King of Kent in AD 664. He was worried that the two nephews of the Abbess, Ethelred and Ethelbert, also had claims to the throne. He had them brutally murdered. The hit-man was one of those shadowy counsellors behind the throne, a man called Thunor. Later Egbert repented of his sins and by law he had to pay *wergild*, the blood-debt, to Aebbe. This should have been gold, but the saintly lady hit on an original scheme. She wanted land from the King for a religious order.

The Saxons had strange ways of fixing a land boundary. Sometimes it would be as far as a man could throw his battleaxe. She wanted more, so it was agreed that the boundaries would be set as far as her pet doe could run. Thunor tried to dissuade the King from giving up his land. He probably coveted it himself. The King remained adamant; the day was set. The doe was released and scampered off, but Thunor leapt on to his horse and set off in pursuit of the doe with evil designs in mind. Suddenly the earth opened up and swallowed him. He was never seen again. It was God's judgement, they said. I have searched in vain for 'Thunner's Leap'. Realistically, I am searching for a fosse. The last mention of it I came across was in a book, *A Dictionary of Saintly Women* by Agnes Dunbar (1904).

So, I combined two hobbies, fishing the gravy-brown Wantsum for bream, and walking. In the noonday heat, having secreted my gear in a ditch, I stroll the ancient droves in search of what must have been a deep fosse into which Thunor's horse stumbled. These droves follow the old routes by which the men of Thanet moved their livestock across these marshes. So far I have been disappointed. The place name seems to have left human consciousness. The Grey Men's concrete has been laid in our minds.

*... the contemplative man's recreation ...*
*– Izaak Walton's Compleat Angler*

It's trite, I know, this familiar quotation. Yet it implies cruelty. It gives the same advice as that of the ancient Oracle at Delphi. 'Know thyself.' Who can face up to that truth? It is akin to staring into the face of the sun.

If you read a book on cosmology, for example Hawking's *A Brief History of Time*, you discover a contradiction about the nature of the Universe. Einstein's theories of relativity are provable. Planck's Quantum Theory is provable. Both are true, but as yet irreconcilable, one with the other. Hawking tells us that when the two theories are reconciled we will understand the mind of God. It so confuses me that I feel like climbing into the box with Schrödinger's cat.

When writing this book I came across the incompatibility between two apparent truths which I discussed earlier. The first was Sartre's dictum that 'Man is condemned to be free'. The second was William Sargant's claim that every decision we make is predetermined, therefore not freely made. You see why I have so much trouble with philosophy and why dear old Izaak would like to tie my brain into knots? Is this why I adopted fishing as a way of life, to escape from those agonies of decision in Sartre's world of existentialism?

My problems are that from the age of eleven I have questioned nearly everything that I have been told by priests and politicians. I do not respect Authority. Nor do I wish to maintain standards. These are the virtues of the middle class. I prefer to share a rusty mug of *vin rouge* with a bearded anarchist *costaud* in the Place de la Bastille. You will have guessed that I am sceptical about the teachings of orthodox religion, and yet I am drawn to old churches.

On our honeymoon my wife and I found the river Torridge too low to fish. We strolled along one of those hedgerow-bound lanes which Chesterton's English drunkard would have rolled along, years ago. We were seeking a lake at Shepbear which our landlord had stocked with Loch Leven trout, famed for being as silver as grilse and as powerful as a village blacksmith. We tired of the fishing under the noonday sun. Some village lads had plunged into the water to cool themselves. My eyes wandered towards a church in the neighbouring grounds of a private estate ... presumably the property of the Lord of the Manor in days gone by. We climbed the gate and entered.

What was it that captivated me? Immediately I was struck by the coolness of the nave under the high roof. The old stones chilled the air. There was a musty smell, a mixture of beeswax on the woodwork and parchment from the books. A mottled imagery of blue, gold and red splotches was projected onto the pews as the light streamed through the stained-glass windows. I smiled at the scene in such a window; a row of bearded saints were sitting at a table, the legs of which were firmly planted in the clouds. Winged angels were swooping towards them to serve them a celestial lunch.

There, on the top of a tomb, were the medieval knight and his lady, a pet hound at their feet. The mighty sword was firmly clutched between the warrior's mailed fists as if he were ready to step down and do battle with any fiends which dared to invade his holy resting place. There were saintly ladies, too, always clad in virgin-white gowns which were so delicately sculpted in marble that I expected their skirts to ruffle ... seemingly they were awarded equality in Heaven when at that time they would have been denied the parson's pulpit and the bishop's palace here on Earth. I smiled, too, at the thought that long ago there might have been monks nearby who would not have thought it sinful to winkle out a carp or two from the lake to grace their platters on the meatless Fridays.

The association of ideas is strange, for I felt so frustrated that I was fingertip-close to the world of those people, and still shut away from them by time. It was much like that tantalising 'turn of the screw' as described in that horrific tale by Henry James. It is a screw being turned in a wall dividing two rooms, the room beyond being unknown, unseen, but the point of the screw enters it. The man who drives it cannot see what the screw would have seen had it not been sightless. Is this not phenomenonalism? Is this why a fisherman seems to find far more ghosts in his lonely haunts than the busy money-hunting town dweller? I believe in ghosts. I have heard far too many tales by anglers whose honesty I respect to discount them. Apart from the invisible footsteps I heard and described earlier there was one personal experience I had which was beyond the material world.

My mother was ill in hospital. I had to pass the hospital on my way to the trout fishery I was managing at that time. When I arrived at the ward her bed was empty. The nurse told me that she was progressing well. She had been taken to X-ray, and she would be sent home soon. Reassured, I continued on to the lake and rowed out to enjoy fly fishing in the calm afternoon. I began to feel uneasy. Suddenly the certainty came into my mind that my mother had died. I stopped fishing and drove home. My son told me that the hospital had rung to say that my mother had passed away ...

Of course we always associate ghosts with the supernatural. Yet, if I cannot reject them, how do I reconcile the stories I hear from honest folk with Huxley's humanist dictum, that all phenomena are explicable in naturalistic terms? For if I have a God it must be a scientific force whose natural laws are miracles enough, without magic. We associate ghosts with places, like the cottage on the Lower Mertoun beat of Tweed. I believe that it is not the place that is haunted. I think the phantom is in the brain of the person who goes to that place and he projects it in front of his own eyes. He sees it there. He is unaware that he brought it with him in his unconscious mind. He passes it on to other receptive minds. And that is my definition of 'being psychic' ...

... and yet this does not satisfy. Here I am in memory. I have left my cottage by the sea to stroll down to the beach at Bonchurch. I have my long rod and tripod under one arm. My mongrel dog, Chester, is on a lead held in my other hand. We have to pass the portal of an ancient church. Chester stops. His legs become rigid, his paws dragging in the dust. His eyes are wide with fear and all his hair has started up. I have to drag him whimpering, past that place near to where Swinburne told us '*no life lives for ever; dead men rise up never ...*' But beyond the church Chester regains his composure, his hair lies flat, his tail wags from side to side. He will soon be leaping excitedly into the surf as I bring in another monster sand-dab.

So, what is this fishing life about? It is about escapism. And we all need to escape from time to time, the fearful ones like me more often than others. This was the philosophy of the anglers of old. Simply speaking, they needed the peace, to be by the water. Everything has changed. Although some of us still seek the wilderness, we have to admit that angling has to match society. Many a modern angler cannot enjoy the pleasure of loneliness. He turns angling into a social sport. Time is money, even by the river and lake. He was born to compete within a competitive society. He takes his anxiety and stress into his fishing life. He has to fish in company. He has to beat the others.

He comes off the water after a competition, his eyes reddened with concentration and his head pounding. His nerves are screwed up to breaking point as they weigh the fish. He has not escaped. Yes, he has taken his own ghosts with him onto the water.

Or there's the lager-saturated bivvy-boy, snoring the night away whilst his self-hooking carp-lines fish on their own. When the scarlet Cyclops-eye glows and the electronic alarm clamours, he staggers to the rod, still fuddled with sleep, and he horses in a gut-bucket carp which is too grotesque to fight. He has not escaped. Bartok's piano concertos may have captured the mysterious sounds of the dark, the whirring of insects, the croak of a frog; he knows them not. He has landed lip-scarred Fred for the umpteenth time; there is no mystery in the lake.

On rare occasions the veil of Time is rent by the tip of a fishing rod. The tale was told by that master of the short story, de Maupassant. It is the siege of Paris in 1870. The Prussian army has bottled in the citizens, but two fishermen know a secret way to the river. They sneak through the enemy lines. They catch a nice mess of gudgeon for their *friture*. They are unlucky. They are caught on their way back. They are accused of being spies. The two old *copains* are shot and the firing squad enjoys the gudgeon fry-up.

Nearer to our own time, the Polish roach-pole fishermen are watching their floats in the river. They try to ignore the slick of greasy black smoke streaming upwards from a distant chimney. In the evening, as usual, a small boat passes them on its way downstream. There are two black-uniformed guards of the *Totenkopfverbände* escorting two young boys carrying sacks. They are taking the lads down to a meadow to collect grass and groundsel for the pet rabbits of their own children. An angler suddenly cries out: 'Why don't you take the kids back to their mums?' One of the guards laughs sardonically, and replies: 'Don't worry. They'll be joining their parents soon enough.'

Perhaps angling had the last laugh as a dear old fly fishing friend of mine, whilst serving in the army in Germany, was given the duty of escorting the notorious Irma Grese to keep her appointment with Jack Ketch at Shepton Mallet. She was the handsome young blonde who strolled between the huts of the Concentration Camp, Alsatian dog on leash and whip in hand. It's funny; escape from the world as we might, fishing has this ironic trick of confronting us unexpectedly with history. Perhaps there never has been any possibility of escape. We can try. We must face up to Life, draw down deep inside ourselves for those hidden resources of the human spirit, or as Nietzsche would put it, to find the Triumph of the Will . . . not to cross over to his Superman; he doesn't exist. The real challenge is to confess that after all, we anglers, we are as other men. Our fishing rods do not set us apart. True, 'the wind on the heath' beckons us, but sooner or later we must return to those intolerable streets.

# 20

# End Game

*Souviens-toi que le Temps est un joueur avide*
*Qui gagne sans tricher à tout coup! C'est la loi.*
*Le jour décroît; la nuit augmente; souviens-toi!*
*Le gouffre a toujours soif; la clepsydre se vide.*
— Charles Baudelaire, l'Horloge

I remember a summer's evening long ago. Colin Cowdrey, Captain of the County cricket side had brought his team to play a friendly match against our Club. With a pint of beer in his hand he was standing with us behind the veranda of our pavilion.  One phrase of his conversation stuck in my mind. 'I count myself amongst the luckiest of men to play cricket in Kent. Not only is it a beautiful County but the Kentish folk are mad about cricket. It's nice to live here.' As our team's leg-spin bowler I was angry with him. I knew he wanted to lose his wicket. His visit was a busman's holiday so he skied each of my deliveries high into the air. Each catch was dropped by our butter-fingered fielders. What came to my mind was when Bradman first appeared at the Oval. The bowler was hoping to become captain of the England team. Bradman drove him to all corners of the field. A  wag called out to the bowler, 'Don't worry, mate! You've got him in two minds. He doesn't know whether to hit each

220

ball for a four or a six!' At the end Cowdrey stood one side to let a ball hit his wicket.

Years later when my wife and I began house hunting all over Britain to find our retirement home neither of us were sad to leave the County we once loved. I reflected that there was hardly one Kentish fishery where I could not hear the thunder of car-wheels on the new motorways. The absence of black spot fungus on my rose bushes was not due to my gardening skill. The air was too polluted by car exhaust fumes to allow the fungus spores to survive. A curiosity. In woodland near our home elm trees were thriving when disease blighted them across Britain. It was believed that car exhaust fumes from nearby gridlocked traffic protected them.

Having been evicted from our family home as innocent casualties of domestic break-up, in 1952 my mother and I bought a large Edwardian house where we could furnish a granny flat for her ageing parents. The house stood in a quiet lane. Our fresh milk was supplied by a working farm some quarter of a mile away.

Our lane was discovered as an alternative route to London. By the time we left in 2006 it was gridlocked with traffic by morning and evening. On windless days the fumes stung in our eyes. It was time to go. I had two favourite fishing places where I could escape artificial put-and-take fishing for stocked trout. For some thirty years I had alternated my fishing holidays between Upper Teesdale and Caithness. Distance ruled out the Flow Country. We found an enchanting cottage attached to a redundant church in a small village, Lartington, near Barnard Castle. It was the Priest's house in former times. It was said that the difference between the two main churches was that Anglican Priests had better halves but Catholic priests had better quarters. Our Priest had been a Catholic so the cottage was his castle. Out of sorts one day, I stamped in from the garden. My wife enquired what had upset me. 'Damned black spot on the roses!' I told her.

I have to warn you now that writing sometimes imposes dilemmas on the author. Such a dilemma descended on me by accident. It was due to a message from a distant third cousin of the Bucknall clan. She was researching the family tree. She asked if she could call on us to garner our memories. We welcomed her. She presented us with a scroll showing my family predecessors right back to the 18th Century. I was mildly excited. Due to parental separation I knew little of my father's family other than that they owned Heyop House where the first Axminster carpets had been made. The truth was that my Bucknall ancestors could hardly have been a more boring set of people. They lived in rural Lincolnshire, perhaps taking their name from the village of Bucknall. I knew there were famous Bucknalls elsewhere. Field Marshal Montgomery had sacked a General Bucknall because he was reluctant to attack the historical City of Caen after D Day. If, when the war was over you had visited the heap of rubble which was Caen after being saturated by bomb and shell, you might have had some sympathy for the errant General. Then a certain Tony Bucknall was briefly captain of our National Rugby team. Alas, he did not last long in that position. Neither of these notable Bucknalls was in my blood-line.

If I were hoping for some exciting forebears, maybe a highwayman or a rebel against society, I would be disappointed. These Lincolnshire Bucknalls were farm-workers, generation after generation. My cousin Sue could discover only one of them who owned some land. There was the occasional baby born on the wrong side of the blanket. To their credit the families cared for these illegitimate Bucknalls whose parents never discovered the wonders of modern science which we call contraception. French Letters were for foreign correspondents.

I should now reveal a little more about the identity of my long-time friend known to readers by his non-de-plume, Jack-by-the Hedge. In 1941 he was a fellow pupil at Maidstone Grammar School. Though we were in different classes we sometimes met on the village bus. My journey to school was ten miles each way. His family lived in the wing of a Tudor manor house not far from Yalding. The coat-of-arms of the Vane family was displayed in the big hall. After our own home was bombed in 1944 his family offered us temporary accommodation until we could return home.

What were risibly termed 'First Aid Repairs' were applied to houses which were only partially destroyed. They consisted of our windows being replaced with tar-coated canvas. Internal walls were rebuilt with Breeze-Blocks. They were plastered over with pink Keene's Cement. Doors which were blown out would be replaced the other way round where the lintels were still sound. Great gaps in ceilings were replaced by a mixture of plaster and straw called Donkey's Breakfast. It made a lovely squelching sound when it flopped onto the floor. Much of this work was done by Irish labourers who ran the risk of Goering's ire to earn work and wages they could not find at home. Whilst most of their work was crude some was so expertly done that years after the war home-owners found it unnecessary to do it again. There were skilled craftsmen in their ranks. What was disconcerting was when the engine of a Flying Bomb stuttered and stopped overhead the family would find their air-raid shelter shared with a number of frantic Irishmen. So my mother and brother would occupy the back rooms of our house in West Wickham. In the summer holidays of 1944 I was rehoused with a farm-working family in the rural village of Horsmonden, not too far from Tonbridge. Martin and I were still able to fish together as our homes were now only a few miles apart.

Years passed. We lost touch. In the sixties I bumped again

into Martin. We were both watching a motor-cycle dirt-track competition at the sparsely populated village of Wormshill, high on the North Downs. The village Church of St. Giles had been built on the site of a pagan temple. The name of Wormshill is thought to be a corruption of 'Woden's Hill' where invading Norsemen settled. The village pub was renowned for its thirst-quenching vintage cider. Martin owned a house in the Weald. It was said to have been built where a medieval Priory had been  despoiled by Thomas Cromwell who owned a manor at nearby Frittenden.

Martin was interested in writing and its techniques. I told him that I was being pressed to write my autobiography. He was critical of my intention to write 'a sunny book of angling reminiscences'. Under his pen-name I published some of Martin's own tales in the Newsletter of the Kent branch of the Salmon & Trout Association. We cooked up his wild-flower pen-name. He reminded me that his employers did not allow their staff to write for public consumption. He advised me that my life-story should include the sad as well as the glad, or it would not be true to life. I had described my coming book figuratively as a stroll down a sunny country lane. He insisted that I should also let the shadows fall across the way. We discussed some of those shadows. I told him about the death of my Barnhill school-friend. I promised Martin that if the opportunity came I would try to find the sexual predator, the headmaster of Barnhill School, Philip Austin who was suspected of abducting and killing Tony in 1944.

I reminded Martin that he had met Tony once in high summer of that quiet year of 1943 when we cycled down into the Weald for a day's fishing to meet Martin by a farm pond which I knew was inhabited by superb roach.

We used to cycle everywhere. Strangely enough, from Bromley to the Weald by bike, it is nearly all downhill. I had discovered a return country-lane route via the Crays along which we sneaked back-home through the River Darent valley. By leaving before sun-up, we could have several hours of fishing and yet reach home before dark.

It was not until 2012 that Sue provided me with the evidence about Austin's subsequent criminal career ... I thought it would be sufficient to allow me to appeal to the Attorney General to set aside the 1944 Inquest verdict of Natural Causes and replace it with Unlawful Killing. She had volunteered to go to the newspaper archives at Colindale to search for reports of any criminal activity in his name. I reminded her that she would be looking for a man who used the third of his Christian names, Philip. His full name was Allen George Philip Austin. Funny thing, I remembered seeing his full name on a document at Barnhill School. It lingered in my mind because it is also a Bucknall family tradition to use preferentially second Christian names. I also recollected that Austin's family home was alone with his mother in Liverpool. I asked her to search in local papers in the North West.

It was a simple equation. If there were no criminal reports of AGP Austin then I would accept the 1944 Inquest verdict of Misadventure ... I was gobsmacked when Sue sent me press reports from the year 1967/8.

A man called AGP Kelly had been arrested in Liverpool. He was brought back to Blackpool 'to help the Police with their enquiries.' Whilst being held in custody he swallowed sodium cyanide to kill himself. A Police Public Statement was held where the Detective Chief Inspector stated that Kelly's name was also AGP Austin who had five previous convictions for sexual assault on victims three of whom had been drugged.

Here was my dilemma. These reports allowed me to make further enquiries to be compiled in a file to be submitted to the Attorney General. If I included all of it in this revised second edition of my autobiography it would have two effects which I believe would spoil this book. I would have had to change my writing style to one of plain reporting. The biographer's aim is to entertain readers. There is neither humour nor angling interest in the sordid story of tracking down a homicidal sex pervert.

The second problem for me was to include this important episode without letting it dominate. After all, in 1944 the RAF was incinerating women and children by fire-bombing German Cities. Hitler's minions were stuffing Jewish women and children into gas chambers. So why become obsessed with one falling leaf in the forest? Original Sin was evenly distributed. A Special Constable upbraided Air Marshal Harris for speeding in his car during the black-out. 'You might kill somebody,' he said. The head of Bomber Command replied testily, 'Young man, I kill hundreds every night!'

What happened in 1944? In September schools in SE London were evacuated due to the devastation by rocket and flying bomb. Evacuation was not compulsory. Barnhill staff and pupils went to North Wales. Tony's family were offered accommodation in Welwyn Garden City. Austin had been living in an apartment at Barnhill School. He was befriended by the Ganley family who lived close by. They invited him to share their Sunday dinner at their home.

Austin arrived unexpectedly at the Ganley family's residence in Welwyn on Saturday 16th September. He invited Tony to cycle over next morning to meet him at the railway station of St. Albans to collect some pellets for his air pistol. Tony set off on his bike early next morning. His parents had no idea he was going to meet Austin. They believed that he had gone for a bike ride. He promised to return for lunch. He did not return. They would never again see him alive. Four days later his body was found on grassland close to Dulwich College where Austin used to teach part-time. Tony's head was buried in the ground. He died from suffocation. Austin also disappeared. Austin did not attend the first two Inquests at Southwark which had to be postponed.

Austin attended the third Inquest summons at Southwark. He claimed that Tony had met him as planned, collected the air-gun pellets and cycled away. Austin then gave an account of his confused travelling over the intervening days whilst suffering from amnesia. He knew he had been to Betws-y-Coed where his school was evacuated. Coincidentally, boys and staff of Dulwich College Preparatory school were also evacuated to the same place at that time. Austin claimed he also went to his family home in Liverpool, to Crewe, Bristol and Glasgow. He recovered his memory and returned to London to the Inquest. Probably because he had been recognised there, he made the damaging admission that he had been sleeping in Dulwich College over the two day period when Tony's body was discovered nearby.

The pathologist Keith (CR) Simpson testified that Tony died from suffocation. The buried head and considerable bruising on knees, mouth, legs, body parts, cheek bones and hands were due to the violent stage of an epileptic fit ... The tongue was bitten through which in those days was recognised as symptomatic of an epileptic fit. The pathologist claimed that Tony buried his own head in the ground, blocking his air-ways, so he suffocated. We do not know if Simpson saw the body *in situ* or at the mortuary. The press report does not mention a toxicological investigation so probably there was none. As the Coroner sat without a Jury it seems probable that there was a pre-Inquest verdict agreed between the police, the pathologist and the Coroner. This is normal; it is not conspiratorial. The Coroner has to decide whether or not to empanel a jury.

A detective sergeant gave evidence that he viewed the body and saw no signs of foul play such as a ligature or binding ...

Staff, neighbours and parents attending the Inquest were hoping at least for an Open Verdict. They disbelieved the one given. This is why the Ganley family has been so supportive of my appeal. I did my best for them though figuratively I felt disorientated in the Corridors of Power. I have not read enough Kafka.

The 1968 Inquest on the death of a young lorry driver in a Blackpool sea-front flat named Philip Austin as the man's killer (Guardian, 22nd November, 1968). Two men met Austin in a local pub. The three men then went to the sea-front flat which Austin had booked short-term. One of these men, Duffy, was blindfolded, drugged and sexually assaulted. When he recovered his senses he found himself alone except for the naked body of the other young man on the bloodstained bed. The dead man had been bound and strangled with considerable force. Austin had left the scene.

I explain briefly why the jury chose an Open Verdict. Partial strangulation is sometimes used by sado-masochists to enhance the effects of an erotic experience though that would exclude 'great force'. Either way, the Jury named Austin as being responsible for the young man's death.

The Police later arrested Austin in Liverpool. He was brought to Blackpool Police station where he committed suicide with Cyanide. A camera in Austin's possession showed photographs only of the dead victim. Chief Detective Inspector Gordon Bailey said that of Austin's previous five convictions he had given chloroform or drugs to three men before sexually assaulting them.

Physical evidence, which is still arriving, satisfied me that the 54 year old '1968 Austin' was the same man as the 31 year old Austin who for a short time was accepted as Headmaster of Barnhill School for Boys in 1943/4.

Samuel Duffett, that patient, courteous and even sympathetic Civil Servant at the Attorney General's office replied by letter to my appeal on 4th July, 2013. I believe that over the next six months the appeal was treated seriously.

I was not surprised when the appeal did not succeed. The killer punch was simply that the record of the 1944 Inquest could not be found – An Inquest record which does not exist officially cannot be challenged ... so that is that! After all, I understand that the Queen refuses to allow DNA tests on the remains of the two young lads who were found buried under a staircase in the Tower of London. They are thought to be the bones of the two sons of Edward IV, suffocated on the orders of their ruthless Uncle, Richard III. Yet Richard's bones, found underneath a car park in Leicester, were subject to scientific tests and verified.

Sam Duffett also gave me other reasons why the appeal would not have succeeded even if the Inquest report had been found by the Chief Coroner at Southwark and/or if the Philip Austin of 1944 had been identical to the Philip Austin of 1968. Many of his arguments for Status Quo would be open to challenge had the report been found. Some Inquest proceedings were reported in copper-plate hand-writing in those days as were my father's bank-statements.

I realised that Press reports of the time gave grounds for serious doubts of the testimonies, but they were inadequate for the Attorney General to persuade the High Court to set aside that 1944 Verdict. Reluctantly I accepted this fact. Yet when facing a future when Politicians seek to institute secret trials, secret inquests, secret enquiries, secret surveillance, incarceration without defence or trial, I raise a glass to Orwell's perceptive vision of 1984. That year is a long time coming, but it is on its way. All our Political Masters have to do to make Orwellian controls acceptable to the Proles is to create an atomsphere of fear.

Remember those gullible MPs who were hoodwinked by the infamous 'dodgy dossier' and the consequential slaughter that it has caused? Fishing connection? I once saw in a London pub a glass-cased fish caught by officers in the 'Messpot' War long ago. The dear old patriotic *Fishing*

*Gazette* collected tackle to send out to Tommies to that part of the Great War. But in our time our troops were warned not to fish for the famous 'Tigris salmon' as the rivers of Iraq were polluted by putrefying corpses.

I felt uncomfortable fishing with anglers who had been conditioned to being competitive in a sport which over the years had become over-competitive.

The strange thing is that I felt guilty when fishing for trout if I started to catch more fish than my boat partner. I recollect going afloat on Loch Watten when I quickly took four fish before my companion had taken one. He shouted out in frustration, 'Oh I see I am going to be hammered today.' I made an excuse to lay down my rod for a while . . . This enabled him to catch up and peace reigned supreme. I do not set out to catch more fish than other anglers. I cannot relax in the atmosphere of competitive stress. This is one reason why I preferred to fish from the bank rather than in a boat.

Bank fishing suits Toftingall, a relatively shallow loch in the Flow Country. Stretching out in the cotton-grass with a modest cup of 'ardent sperrits' in hand, between the tufts of white fluff on the slender grass stems I can see the pink cone of a wild orchid. An anxious Oyster Catcher is tempting me to follow her away from her nesting site. On the far side of the old-ale water a Black-throated Diver prospects for food. Around midday, even in summer, long after their season has finished in the South, hatching mayflies drift somnolently in the wind-lane which formed within casting distance of my hide in the herbage. Sometimes a brief gust of wind will catch their wing-spinnakers to make them scoot along the surface of the loch. I had discovered a secret of Toftingall. The trout rise a yard or two beyond the oily slick of the wind-lane. Yes, I knew this. The Ospreys did not. The giant eagles arrived for lunch, cruising above the slick water-way signposted by tiny patches of foamy bubbles.

The midges have found me. They stick in the beads of sweat below my hat-band. I drag myself to me feet. I push through the grass-tangle to the edge of the conifer plantation. There are the dark-green shrubs of bog myrtle. They fill the air with their incense.

I crush the foliage and rub the verjuice into my stinging brow. Sprigs are pushed into my hat. I reflect that if Blake told us that 'everything has its vermin,' the medieval monk-herbalist would have replied, 'yes, but God also provided the remedy nearby'.

Whilst I told my friends that I understood why the Queen Mother and her entourage pick-nicked at Toftingall I wondered how they coped with these minute stinging pests. Did they also crush the Bog Myrtle leaves? 'Oh no', they said. 'Gin is also effective.' I wanted to know? Inside or outside? 'Both!' they replied.

So as a good part of my fishing life was in teaching beginners how to dress and cast an artificial fly I believe you will forgive me if I survey some of my contributions to the sport. Surely Octogenarian anglers must have achieved something?

I believe I can claim to be one solver of that frustrating evening rise known as 'the Blagdon Boil'. I can date my successful fly pattern from the year when Newcastle United won the FA cup. Their captain, a man called Loftus, raised the cup for all to see. I noticed the black and white strip he was wearing. 'That's it,' I told the amateur angling photographer, Ron Ward. "Forget Bulls Eye. We will call it 'the Footballer.'" It happened that like the other bank anglers we retrieved our flies through legions of cruising fish which were leisurely sipping down invisible natural insects in the surface film. The general opinion was that the fish were taking minuscule Caenis pupae which were too small to imitate.

Eventually we did catch a trout. We spooned out its stomach contents. There we found a tightly packed boulette of insect protein. We placed this in a dish of water and spread out the massed insects. I asked Ron to photograph them and to enlarge the print. All became clear. The fish were feeding on Chironomidae pupae which were stuck in the thick molecular wall of the surface film. The pupae were hook-shaped, their bodies were alternate narrow bands of black and white. I copied the abdomen with black and white horsehair wound side by side from half-way round the hook-bend over a layer of white tying thread. A pinch of mole's fur was dubbed in at the throat to simulate the thorax. The head was finished off with a turn or two of bronze peacock herl.

The tactic was to grease one's leader down to the point, then to tie onto the point a single small imitation on a size 14 or 16 hook. This buzzer nymph as it was later called had to be fished very slowly indeed. There came to Blagdon an ideal summer's evening. The surface of the lake was the gentlest ripple from what the poet once called a zephyr. The Blagdon Boil was soon frustrating the line of anglers along the Butcombe bank. In desperation most of them speeded up their casting and fly retrieve which was counter-productive. Ron and I both caught four trout each. One or two fishermen came along to discover what fly we were using.

After publishing the story of the Blagdon Boil I began to receive success stories from all over Britain. Today there are myriads of 'skinny nymphs'. Then there were none.

A recent poll on a TV programme decided that my Footballer was the first true copy of the 'buzzer nymph'. So far, touch wood, my claim to 'the Footballer' fame has never been disputed. I have been a Newcastle United supporter ever since.

It was Eric Horsfall Turner who reminded us that we did not invent, we only re-discovered. The most rancorous feuds in our sport have involved the 'who thought of it first?'

syndome. Turning the sere pages of the old *Fishing Gazettes* when researching for my anthology[2] of that great weekly paper I discovered that nearly every claim for an invention was challenged. Even dear old Cannon Greenwell had to defend the famous fly which bears his name. The Black Pennell, the Wickham, the Pheasant Tail Nymph, Kite's Imperial, they were all challenged. I smiled when RS Austin, inventor of Tups Indispensable let it be known that the indispensable component for the thorax dubbing was the wool from a ram's scrotum! I was surprised that he did not make it a bull!

I would turn around Turner's maxim. We do not discover. We only re-invent. It is fair enough if we honestly acknowledge the source of our wisdom. Thus it was with my giant Beastie lure. I was boat fishing on Hanningfield with my surgeon friend, Tony Richards. The boat was positioned to lie athwart the broad and oily wind-lane we nicknamed the M1. With the light shining along it, we could see shoals of rainbow trout humping through the surface as they cruised upwind towards us. I was astonished when Tony clipped a large lead shot (allowed in those days) onto the shank of a sizeable black lure. 'Just watch!' He said. 'You have to be accurate to drop your lure just ahead of an approaching fish. The lure stays a second on the surface, and then it dives down. You should see the fish disappear from the surface to follow the lure.'

Matching word to deed Tony dropped his lure nicely before the eyes of an advancing rainbow. The fish did vanish from the surface. As Tony started to retrieve the lure the savage 'take' by the trout nearly tore the rod from his hand. At the fly-tying bench I *believed* that I could improve on Tony's lure by fashioning it into a modern version of that traditional Edwardian 'eel tail'. I added for its wings two

---

[2] *The Bright Stream of Memory*, Swanhill 1997.

whole black marabou tips with cheeks of silver pheasant flank feathers and jungle cock. I weighted it with two turns of lead wire at the head. I reasoned that the bulk of the marabou would allow me to fish this lure on a sinking line. It was curious to see that the lure was nearly always lodged at the back of the trout's throat. Again, reports flowed in of successes to my Beastie lure until in its turn it was eclipsed by Trevor Housby's simpler Dognobbler lure.

I should have had a success with a personal sea-rod design. Trouble is that rod designs cannot be patented effectively. I do not know who first invested staggered ferrules in fly rods. The idea is to make the top rod section longer than the butt ... I thought this would be ideal if it could be applied to the light rods on my boat, Cygnus M when casting up-tide in estuarine waters of the Thames basin. I was able to reduce the overall rod length to 9 feet with a longer top section which would bend over nicely to lock the lead weight into the sea-floor. It worked efficiently. I was remiss in not commercialising it through my firm Sundridge Tackle. I wanted to hug it to myself and to boast of it when friends clambered aboard the boat carrying their usual 10 to 12 foot bass rods. My personal rod vanished from my boat. An identical design later appeared in the catalogue of a rival company, bearing the name of its 'inventor', a former friend of mine. Staggered ferruled rods were not uncommon so I had no complaints whilst remembering that Spanish proverb, '*amigo reconciliado, enemigo doblado.*'

I moved Cygnus M away from the Essex coast.

Authors who resorted to self-publishing were thought to be those whose manuscripts had been rejected by orthodox publishers. This is not true. Writers who wish to publish their own works can choose between many specialised firms who will help them. There are many reasons why authors prefer to publish their own work.

My own choice for self-publishing was due to my dissatisfaction with one or two previous publishers. I always wished to be involved with the production planning of my books. My first publisher, Frederick Muller laid on a special conference to which the author and his illustrator were invited. The book editor would discuss such important questions as paper quality, choice of type-face, number and size of illustrations. The Sales Manager would explain the firm's policy on advertising, publicity and freebie copies for review and how the author might help to promote sales. I was amazed that the *Daily Worker* favoured Muller's books. I bit my tongue as I knew that the owner of that paper had abandoned his Russian wife for her to be sent to one of Stalin's Gulags. He did nothing to save her. It was Tom Driberg MP who secured her release and passage to Britain. Even so, my 'Muller' books about the Capitalist image of fly fishing received warm praise in the *Daily Worker*. I felt guilty on seeing a communist cousin of mine selling the *Daily Worker* on Victoria Station; I turned up my collar and sneaked past her to catch my train.

When Swanhill published my books the illustrator, Aideen Canning and I were invited to their offices in Shrewsbury, again to be consulted in the production planning conference. The third book I wrote for Swanhill was a disaster. Their experienced Managing Director, Alastair Simpson had died suddenly of cancer, though still of no great age. His widow decided to keep the business afloat. She asked the regular angling writers to produce the standard text books which brought a quick return on investment. I wrote for her a comprehensive book on fly fishing for brown trout.[3] The new editor did not invite me to sit in on production planning meetings – if there were any.

When the proofs arrived I was horrified to see that my

---

[3] *Fly Fishing Tactics for Brown Trout* (Swanhill, 2000)

beautiful colour pictures had been reproduced in black and white – or should I say in shades of grey? I had been proud of the written text I sent him for the book. I was deeply ashamed by the art-work in the finished product. It was awful. He excused the drab photographs as cost cutting necessity. Paradoxically I received many friendly letters from readers of that book even though review copies were not sent out because the firm was already being wound up.

One reviewer of the First Edition of this book said that the book trade must be in deep recession if recognised authors like me had to resort to self-publishing. This was not the reason for my choice. I thought it would be fun to publish my own book. I set myself up as a one-man company, *the Bright Water Press*. That is a lovely name I would be happy to pass it on gratuitously to another self-publisher.

The temptation is to print more copies than you can sell. The firms which help self-publishers return the disc with the whole book on it, so further copies can be produced at any time. I decided to produce an enlarged and revised second edition as two major issues had arisen from the First Edition. They had to be answered.

The problem for self-publishing authors is selling the product. I am too arthritic now to trail from bookshop to bookshop. We need the wholesale book trade to support self-publishing authors, given that the quality of the product is good. Hilaire Belloc described himself ... 'his sins were scarlet but his books were read.' And a profit margin must be included to attract the wholesale trade. Yet the wholesale trade must come up with a policy to accommodate authors who prefer to publish their own work. In their retail outlets they could set aside a section to display and promote such products. This subject is important to me as I know several good angling writers who now produce their own books. The shrinking book market is paradoxically the saviour of what has been called unkindly 'vanity publishing'.

So now as the shadows fall I recall with sympathy those words of Viscount Grey in his book simply entitled *Fly Fishing*. He was losing his eyesight, much like my old friend Kenneth Robson, both victims of macular degeneration. Grey had the sad vision of all the lights of Europe going out as war came.

It is rewarding to know that our sport meshes in with our own experience of life. Being perhaps the last Europhile in Britain I loved to fish across that patchwork quilt of contrasting landscapes and cultures which make up our continent. Images flash across the screen of memory. My float goes under the surface of the large lake near Dieppe. My friend Henri hands me the rod. 'Here, Rosbif, strike it! Your first French pike!' And now Manfred in Austria is pushing my legs into a tight pair of thermal waders. 'Don't face upstream as you would in England. This mountain torrent will knock you over. Go downstream with the flow'. Susan has taken me to spin for garfish in the sea off Denmark ... 'we have so many fish to carry home. We must stack them in our waders and walk barefoot to the car.' Olof is leaning over the stern of his boat. We are off Marstrand. He is waving his gaff excitedly. 'There's a great halibut coming up for the cod you have hooked. I can see it, deep down. Stop winding, Geoff. It will take your cod'. Then a Swedish swear word ... 'ah, he's seen the light and dived away. About a hundred of your English pounds in weight.' I remembered Ernie Bevin's ambition as Foreign Secretary ... 'that I can walk to Victoria Station and buy a train ticket to anywhere'. I would add this. 'Don't forget your fishing rod, Ernie'. Fishing rods and xenophobia do not mix.